FIT
for
PURPOSE

Your Guide to Better Health,
Wellbeing and
Living a Meaningful Life

Harper*Inspire*, an imprint of
HarperCollins Christian Publishing
1 London Bridge Street
London SE1 9GF

www.harpercollins.co.uk

First published by HarperCollins 2021.
Copyright © Dr Richard Pile

Japanese version of Ikigai (page 234) used with permission.
Copyright Nicholas Kemp, Akhiro Hasegawa.

A catalogue record for this book is available from the British Library

ISBN: 9780310124740 (TPB)
ISBN: 9780310124764 (Audio)
ISBN: 9780310124757 (ebook)

Set in Zilla Slab by e-Digital Design

Printed and bound in the UK by CPI Group (UK) Ltd, Croydon CR0 4YY

MIX
Paper from responsible sources
FSC   FSC™ C007454

FIT
for
PURPOSE

Your Guide to Better Health,
Wellbeing and
Living a Meaningful Life

DR RICHARD PILE

INSPIRE

To my family.

Beccy, this book would not have been possible without you. Thank you for your sacrifice, support, encouragement and for keeping it real. I love you.

Josh, Finn and Zac (aka Princes to Kings), I am proud of you; proud of who you are now and who you are on your way to becoming. Being your father has made life truly meaningful, enjoyable . . . and expensive.

Luke, no matter how difficult life may be, you live it to the full. You are the inspiration for this book, for our family and for every life you touch. Or to put in in your own words, you are awesome.

Contents

Introduction

Do you feel well? Are you satisfied with your life?

How do you measure this? Which areas are important to you?

Do you have the right balance of physical, mental, social, and spiritual wellbeing?

Would you like to be living life better? If so, what would that look like to you?

Have you already gone cross-eyed, developed a headache, and are now wondering whether you might have made a mistake starting this book? Were you hoping for more answers, preferably in digestible bullet points, with rather less in the way of questions? Don't worry. You haven't made a mistake. The very fact that you are reading this and contemplating these big questions means that you are already in the right place and heading in the right direction.

What can you expect from this book?

This book will not change your life. Not by itself. Not if you just read it and put it on the bookcase along with all the other books about wellbeing, faith, or self-improvement that are already gathering dust. This book will help you to change your life . . . if you read, reflect, and act on it.

This book is for you and for everyone. It's short, it's simple and pragmatic. It doesn't require you to have lots of time or money, or a degree in medicine or theology. It's practical, with advice and tips on making plans for achievable goals on your journey through life and in faith.

This book is going to challenge some of the behaviours and beliefs that we see, both in society generally and in the faith community specifically.

Finally, this book will leave you asking more questions of yourself and your community as, together, we consider what it truly means to be *fit for purpose*.

1. A Confession

I'm going to start by coming clean: between you and me, I don't read many Christian books. I've tried for over thirty years. I find a lot of them very preachy. I've met some of the authors, who were even more preachy than their books. I can't relate. These people have it all figured out – or seem to at least. They often come across as a bit smug, a bit holier-than-thou. Some of these books do have things of interest hidden within their pages, but finding them is like panning for gold and I'm often left vaguely, but only briefly, interested as they aren't immediately applicable to my own life. Some authors are rather too fond of the sound of their own voices.

When I was a student in Nottingham, I used to attend a very well-known church with a large student congregation. The pastor had a reputation for exegesis (explaining and interpreting biblical text) and had written a book, which he plugged shamelessly at church services. He once preached for almost an hour on two words from a Bible verse. Some people might view this as something of an achievement. For me, it was the straw that broke the camel's back. I took the view that if, as a preacher, you couldn't get to the point in fifteen minutes, particularly when based on so little material, then you probably needed to rethink your life.

Don't get me wrong. There are a handful of books that have had a really positive impact upon my life and faith. What was it about these books? They either told an inspiring story (*The Cross and the Switchblade; Run Baby Run; God's Smuggler*), were really practical and made memorable points that I could translate into real life (*Too Busy Not to Pray*),[1] or made challenging or controversial points (*Velvet Elvis; The God Delusion; God's Undertaker*).[2] And yes, the more observant among you will note that I did just credit Richard Dawkins – God truly does move in mysterious ways. The point of my confession is that I'm making you a promise that I will do my best not to make the same mistakes in this book that put me off reading so many others in the past. I aim to keep it simple, honest, humorous, direct, pragmatic, and personal. Whether I achieve this is, of course, up to you to decide.

As far as I'm concerned, this isn't a Christian book. It's a book about wellbeing and what it means to live a life that's fit for purpose, written by a Christian whose faith, life experience, and clinical expertise inform his understanding of these things. It isn't just for Christians, or for those who consider themselves people of faith. There's plenty here for everyone, with principles that apply to all. There's only one world, the real world, in which I live and work along with everyone else, regardless of our different philosophies. My view of such a world is seen not just through the lens of faith but also experience and evidence, all reflected in the way I have structured it. The book works best if you read it from beginning to end, but I've laid it out so that you will still get something from it if you dip in and out as you wish.

Each chapter describes a different aspect of wellbeing, breaking it down into some narrative about the challenges that we face, the scientific evidence, what we can learn from biblical teaching, and my prescriptions for enjoying greater wellbeing, both as individuals and organizations.

What are my credentials for holding forth on this subject? Why should you be at all interested in what I have to say? My answer would be broadly that I've seen quite a bit of life and feel that there may be some benefit in sharing with others what I've learnt from it. I've spent forty-seven years as a human being, almost a quarter of a century of it as a doctor, over twenty years of which have been as a general practitioner (GP). Thirty-seven years practising my Christian faith. Twenty-six years as a husband, twenty-three years as a father of multiple boys, one of whom has a learning disability and severe epilepsy. A decade of specializing in cardiovascular medicine and providing clinical advice on wellbeing and prevention for various organizations across the UK. Five years or so of dedicating myself to developing a lifestyle-medicine practice, including blogging, podcasting, writing for medical journals and the national press. I think that's sufficient burnishing of my credentials for the time being. Now let's move on to something much more important – I'd like to start by asking you a question.

Notes

1. David Wilkerson with John Sherrill, and Elizabeth Sherrill, *The Cross and the Switchblade* (Old Tappan, 1972); Nicky Cruz and Jamie Buckingham, *Run Baby Run* (Hodder & Stoughton, 2003); Brother Andrew with John and Elizabeth Sherrill, *God's Smuggler* (Hodder and Stoughton, 2008); Bill Hybels, *Too Busy Not to Pray: Slowing Down To Be With God* (IVP, 2011).

2. Rob Bell, *Velvet Elvis: Repainting the Christian Faith* (HarperOne, 2012); Richard Dawkins, *The God Delusion* (Black Swan, May 2007); John Lennox, *God's Undertaker: Has Science Buried God?* (Lion Books, 2009).

2. The Meaning of Wellbeing

What does wellbeing mean to you? Give yourself a moment to consider this question. Have you ever said it out loud or tried to write it down? What does it mean for you to feel well? Are you feeling well right now?

Wellbeing, just like the rest of life, is complicated. The fact that there isn't even a consensus on how to spell it should give you a clue as to where we are when it comes to defining it. Many have tried. A whole industry has sprung out of our attempts to define and even measure it. There are many complex definitions, which you will be pleased to hear I am not going to bore you with . . . not too much, anyway. Many of the definitions aren't even definitions, just lists of possible different components of it.

When some people use the term, they simply mean happiness or quality of life. Others say this is insufficient and it needs to include personal development, feeling fulfilled, and making a contribution to the community. This demonstrates that wellbeing can be subjective (life satisfaction, positive emotions, and meaning), or objective (taking into account factors such as food, health, education, safety, and mortality). How happy we are with our perceived position in life is determined by our culture, values, and experience, in terms of our expectations. It's not just the absence of ill-health.

I think of wellbeing as a state in permanent flux. It's not a static position that we achieve, or a place we finally arrive at and never depart from. It's about balance. Just as we all have mental health, we all experience wellbeing. It's about the amount of challenge we have in our lives and the resources available to us to meet those challenges. Enjoying a positive sense of wellbeing isn't necessarily the same as having it easy, with no challenges to face. The same set of challenges affects people differently. If you have the right resources in your life (physical, social, psychological, and spiritual), then you can endure great challenge and still be in a good place. On the other hand, if you don't have much in the way of personal resources available to you, then it may not take much challenge for you to end up in a bad way. The important thing to remember is that, like stocks and shares, our sense of wellbeing may go up and down. This is good news for us when we are struggling, because it offers hope if we can find a way to shift the balance, and also a caution to anyone who might be feeling a bit smug and taking their state of wellbeing for granted.

One of the reasons that I am a fan of this sometimes tricky, even woolly term is that it can be useful in helping us to de-medicalize what we think of as 'health'; a term that we sometimes think is synonymous with wellbeing, but is in fact just a small part of the bigger picture. Physical and mental health are part of the equation that we need for balance, but they are not the whole story. In fact, what we think of as 'health' is relatively minor to most people when it comes to what determines their wellbeing. It probably accounts for about 20 per cent of it. The rest of life accounts for the other 80 per cent and includes other factors such as our environment, education, relationships, and finances, and our sense of autonomy, purpose, and fulfilment. It's here that we run into difficulties, not with knowledge (most medical practitioners either understand or pay lip service to this truth), but with how we adapt (or rather, fail to adapt) the way we practise medicine as a result.

Why the modern medical model is broken and unfit for purpose

I was going to misappropriate the title of a Blur album and declare that 'modern medicine is rubbish'. That would be a bit of an oversimplification. I'm proud to be a member of the medical profession. Modern medicine can be miraculous, both life-changing and life-saving. There are procedures and treatments available to us now that were mere concepts when I trained at medical school in the 1990s. We can now save lives by busting clots inside the arteries of people's brains and hearts; carry out laparoscopic surgery using tools that mean we no longer have to cut people open; cure or control many kinds of cancer; and give drugs to people with severe inflammatory diseases to reduce the risks of the associated disability and death that would have been considered inevitable once upon a time.

Medicine is, however, just a tool. It's a really fancy, high-tech tool, with more gadgets than a top-of-the-range Swiss Army knife, but it is just a tool. Despite its potential cleverness, in the wrong hands it can be something of a blunt tool, like a hammer. The problem with someone only having a hammer to fix problems is that every problem ends up looking like a nail. The most this fancy tool can do is assist us with up to 20 per cent of what determines our wellbeing. It may well be less for many of us. Just because it will do the job doesn't mean it's the only one, or even the best one, to use. When it comes to addressing the other 80 per cent of what determines our wellbeing, it's at best useless and may even make the problem worse. To persist with the tool analogy for just a little longer, no tool is inherently good or bad. Blaming the medical model is no different from blaming the internet, mobile phones, or social media platforms. It's the uses they are put to that matter. After all, you know what they say about workmen and tools.

What we are faced with is not an equipment failure, it's a user error, a failure to read the manual. Over the last few decades, we have developed a disease-based medical model out of a disease-based mindset. We seek out diagnoses where there aren't any (it's amazing what you can do with some updated definitions of illness that a bunch of experts have decided should exist), and we are incentivized to case-find as if our lives, rather than the pharmaceutical industry's profits, depend on it. We treat ageing as a disease and make herculean efforts to prolong life at whatever cost, unwilling to admit that what really drives us is the fear of death and the assumption that anything that postpones the inevitable must, by definition, be a good thing. We intervene in people's lives because we can, rather than asking ourselves whether we should. We have perpetuated the idea that when a person is broken it is the responsibility of the medical profession to fix them, regardless of the reasons for their being broken to start with. We treat life and its complications with expensive, invasive, sometimes risky interventions, instead of taking the time to explore why these complications of living have arisen and what the best ways are to address them, ideally involving the person concerned. I once had a stand-up row in a meeting with a cardiologist who took issue with the fact that, as health commissioners, we were asking people to attempt to lose weight and stop smoking before major surgery. He accused us of being cruel, despite the fact that there was good evidence that making lifestyle changes would reduce the risks of complications from surgery (including death), improve the outcomes, and in some cases would render the surgery, such as joint replacement, unnecessary. I responded by comparing him to someone standing on a bridge over a river, watching as one person after another floated past him. He was content to fish them out of the water, but didn't show even the slightest bit of curiosity as to why they had all ended up in the river to start with and whether this could have been prevented.

As a doctor I have prescribed antidepressants and painkillers to people whose physical and mental pain is fundamentally due to loneliness, poverty, lack of purpose, and dissatisfaction with life. I have seen people have gastric bypasses who eat because of the pain of their life experiences. I have reluctantly agreed to refer people with multiple, mysterious symptoms to multiple, mystified hospital specialists, because I either don't have the courage to be honest with them about the likely root causes for their malaise, or they are unwilling to contemplate this being something that medicine can't fix. Either way, it gets them out of my consulting room quicker. In the worst case, and sadly not that uncommonly, the specialist will carry out a lot of tests and find an 'incidentaloma' (a coincidental harmless finding unrelated to the original reason for referral), which will open up whole new pathways of probably unnecessary medical or surgical intervention.

I'm not in breach of any guidelines when I practise in this way. In fact, following the latest guidelines from august bodies like NICE (the National Institute for Health and Care Excellence) is more likely to result in my making such referrals and prescribing such medications. I'm not proud of it and nowadays, I try to do much less of it. The problem is that the patient has ended up in front of a doctor with wellbeing-related needs that are, most of the time, not directly related to health. However, due to either a lack of insight into why they don't feel well, or lack of access to the right support, there they are. The doctor then compounds the problem. They do it with the best of intentions, having been trained to try and do whatever they can to help the person in front of them. So, they use the inappropriate tool of the modern medical model. If you think about it for a moment, this is quite bizarre and maybe even unique to medicine. If I was a plumber and the person who called me out actually needed help with their phone, electrics, or pension-planning, I would not attempt to have a go out of the goodness of my heart. I'm not qualified and I'd be likely to make the situation worse. Instead, I'd point them in the right direction. Maybe I would give them the number of someone I would recommend. Sometimes in medical life it is genuinely better to do nothing than something. After all, the Hippocratic oath starts with the principle of first doing no harm.

Many doctors feel like I do, whether they consider themselves advocates of lifestyle medicine or not, but we choose to practise defensive medicine because we are worried that the one time we don't refer the patient to a specialist, and instead offer them lifestyle advice and signpost them to help outside of the medical model, we may miss a serious diagnosis, or (more likely) get a complaint as a result. That's the other part of the problem. We have conditioned our patients in this same model, so their expectations are in keeping with it. It's not their fault. As a result, we spend almost all of our time dealing only with people who are already sick. We know what to do with those people, however ineffectively, because it's what we've trained for. As for the people who are not yet sick (the ones that we don't have time for), we wait helplessly for the inevitable consequences of lifestyle problems to rear their ugly head in the form of chronic disease, and then they become sick too. It is a deeply perverse approach. As doctors we don't do this because we are lazy or bad people. We do it because it's what we have been trained and incentivized to do. I once heard an interview with a doctor who likened the medical system to a cult, because people in it were deprived of sleep and filled with sugar and caffeine until they were too tired to question how it all worked. It requires a real effort, and a willingness to take risks, for us to lift our heads above the parapet and spend time with people addressing the root cause of their problem, and discussing what they can do to take responsibility for themselves and make changes.

Trying to be an authentic practitioner of lifestyle medicine is not without its challenges. Patients may either be delighted or disappointed by such an honest approach. It can take longer to build relationships so that the patient does not feel disappointed, but instead feels encouraged and optimistic that this is something they can take control of. Colleagues may question, or even be opposed to you spending a little more time on this when required. It's not a level playing field in this respect. No one would question giving a double appointment to a patient with a newly diagnosed condition like diabetes, heart disease, or cancer. Yet there can be a frankly baffling reluctance to dedicate a similar amount of time to helping a person avoid developing one of these conditions.

I think part of the problem is that doctors are themselves very expensive and fancy tools, and the question being asked is whether they are the right tool for what seems like a very simple job of talking to someone about their life and how they live it. I agree that as doctors we probably don't need to be involved too often. Nowadays in general practice we are developing teams around us of people who are equipped to help, such as social prescribers and health coaches. There is something powerful, however, about being involved as a doctor at the start of the process, with a patient who trusts you and respects your opinion, and who may be more inclined to buy into making lifestyle changes rather than opting for the traditional disease-based and broken medical model.

And now for the good news . . .

I think I've moaned enough about modern medicine. You probably get the point by now. There is a growing movement in this area in all walks of life, including the medical profession. The *British Medical Journal* has a 'Too much Medicine' series and there are even conferences on the subject. It feels to me that both the public and medical profession are beginning to move slowly in the right direction when it comes to an understanding of what being well really means. People are increasingly willing to accept the importance of the different aspects of our lives that determine our wellbeing, and the foolishness of trying to separate the physical from the mental, the emotional, and the social. This shift in thinking and the issues arising out of it make this book timely. I believe that it is vital we also include the spiritual aspect of our lives. As we work our way through different aspects of what determines how well we feel and how satisfying and meaningful our lives are, I will argue that spirituality is fundamental to our wellbeing, whatever sort of beings we consider ourselves to be.

For now, though, I'd like to start with a story. I've come to understand the power of stories in the last few years. They are the way that we have passed information on to each other for as long as humans have been around on the earth to tell them, which is at least 100,000 years as far as homo sapiens is concerned. Stories are powerful and memorable and a good way of illustrating points. They're much better than PowerPoint presentations, although that is admittedly a pretty low bar. This is my story. Well, thankfully for you, not just my story but, more interestingly, the story of my family.

3. Our Story

At the age of 6, someone asked me what I wanted to be when I grew up. I declared that I was going to be a doctor. When asked why, I couldn't really verbalize it at the time. On reflection, forty years later, I think that I felt it was an important job that would make a difference. It made my path through education quite straightforward. I knew where I was going and what I needed to do to get there. In my teenage years I did some work experience with a family friend who was a GP and, after spending a week shadowing her, I knew that it was what I wanted to do.

We weren't particularly well-off as a family, but after passing an entrance exam and being awarded a bursary, I was fortunate enough to attend one of the best independent schools in the country, Manchester Grammar. It's fair to say the school had very high expectations of its pupils and a lot of those doing sciences for A levels applied to medical school. We were well drilled in preparing for exams and university applications. My only moment of controversy throughout my entire secondary school career was in choosing *not* to apply for Oxford or Cambridge on the grounds that I didn't think I was posh enough and, more importantly, I didn't fancy the extra exams and hard work required to get there.

I was offered a place at each of the five medical schools I applied to, after a series of interviews in which the questions ranged from the obvious ('What would you say are the ten most important scientific discoveries in the last hundred years?') to the bizarre ('So young man . . . the Gulf War. What do you fancy, a home or an away match?'). I chose Nottingham because they threw in an intercalated degree as part of the course, it had a nice green campus, and it boasted a women-to-men ratio of 2:1 – not necessarily in that order of importance.

I was one of the few people at medical school who admitted to wanting to be a GP, despite the fact we all knew full well that about half of us would end up doing exactly that. My research about gender ratios really paid off as I met and fell in love with Beccy, whom I married at the end of my third year at university. I was a mediocre medical student. This was mainly because going to university was a real eye-opener after a strait-laced upbringing, including attending an all-boys secondary school. I was branching out and enjoying the social life a bit more than the actual medicine, including wooing my wife-to-be. I once turned up to a 'viva' (verbal examination) having only revised three out of five systems of the body. The student before me was grilled on haematology (blood) and I was preparing for oblivion and a summer of resits before I lucked out and got asked a neurology (nervous system) question, which I had actually revised for. I appreciate this disclosure may not fill you with confidence in the medical profession, but for what it's worth, you do most of your learning on the job in your career as a doctor!

After graduating from medical school, Beccy and I stayed in Nottingham for my first year as a junior doctor, when I did my surgical and medical house jobs for six months each. It was a gruelling year, but we all knew what to expect and I found it quite enjoyable. I was lucky to bag a job with a world-famous breast surgeon, which I applied for not on the basis of a deep and abiding interest in breast surgery, but because I thought a reference from him would look good on my CV. Halfway through my second job, our son Luke was born. There are probably better times to start a family than halfway through the most difficult year of your entire medical career, but Beccy and I worked well as a team and loved living in our little house in a nearby town. Beccy was on maternity leave from her teaching job, having finished her music degree and then qualified as a teacher. At the end of the year, I applied for a GP training course. I'd like to say it was my brilliance at interview, or the reference from the professor on my CV, that swung it, but it may also have been something to do with the law of supply and demand. When I had applied to the scheme, I rang up to ask when the interviews were, to which the response was – and I quote – 'When can you make it?'

So after finishing my first year as a trainee doctor we moved to beautiful rural Oxfordshire and I continued my training at the Horton District General Hospital in Banbury and did my GP trainee year at a lovely practice in Warwickshire. It was a fantastic year (during which our second son Joshua arrived), and confirmed to me that general practice was the right career for me. After qualifying as a GP, I applied for a job at the surgery where I am a partner today. We moved to St Albans in Hertfordshire and have been there ever since.

So far, so good – or possibly so boring, depending on your view. You're thinking, *Hang on a minute. I've read lots of books about inspirational doctors who set up hand surgeries in Nepal, or risk life and limb on a daily basis working in war zones. Your story is, frankly, a bit on the dull side. Congratulations on overcoming your middle-class struggle, by the way.*

Fair point. However, things are about to get a bit more . . . interesting.

As I've mentioned, Luke is our first child. He was a very happy baby. However, it became apparent that he had some difficulties with communication and interaction. He didn't speak before he was two, and even then his vocabulary was very limited. He tried to compensate for not being able to interact verbally by doing so physically with other children, which they and their parents didn't always understand or appreciate. We wondered if he might be autistic. As it turned out, he wasn't, although he was labelled as that for a while. When we moved to St Albans we had to start from scratch in terms of educational support and get him a statement of special educational needs.

Things didn't go well at his first school. His class teacher was a hideous woman who thought that children with special educational needs were naughty and should be left in a corner of the classroom. She was, ironically, the Special Educational Needs Coordinator, as well as a close friend of the headteacher. We left after two weeks, as we were given the very strong message that his sort weren't welcome, because they dragged down the rest of the class and threatened the school's status as a 'beacon' school. We decided to pick our battles and moved on to another school, which was lovely. The headteacher was very inclusive and although life wasn't straightforward, and not every professional contact was helpful or positive, he thrived in the school and developed at his own pace.

Things changed one day when I got a panicked call from my wife when I was at the surgery. Luke had collapsed suddenly at home. An ambulance had been called. I raced home and arrived as the ambulance did. He was coming round by then, but we agreed to get him checked out in the Accident and Emergency Department (A&E). We were seen by a junior paediatrician who assured us confidently that having a first fit didn't mean that a child was necessarily epileptic (which in fairness is true for most people), and Luke was discharged. As it turned out, Luke was indeed epileptic. The next twelve years of his life were the most difficult time of all our lives. His epilepsy is described as complex and severe. For the first few years, he would have lots of little moments of being absent, known as petit mal seizures, but he also had other sorts of seizures. Monitoring at Great Ormond Street hospital showed he had at least fifty of them a day. The other seizures could be episodes of twitching or sudden collapse (drop attacks). This meant that he could no longer be left alone at any time. We went from being a typical family without much in the way of concerns, other than some learning needs (significant enough for most), to a family on call and on high alert twenty-four hours a day. Either Beccy or I had to be with him all the time when he was at home. As I was at work most of the week, a lot of this fell to Beccy. At night we had to always have a video monitor on. He couldn't ride a bike due to the risk of injury (in the end we bought him a three-wheeler recumbent bike so he would trundle gently to a halt if having a seizure), and he couldn't have a bath. We did let him have swimming lessons, as he was very keen on this and we wanted him to have things in his life that he enjoyed. He wore a life jacket and we spent the next few years watching from the poolside with our hearts in our mouths. I only had to dive in once, fortunately.

Things got a lot worse as adolescence approached and his seizures developed into the grand mal or tonic-clonic type. He would turn his head to one side, grimace, groan, and then go stiff and jerk. Sometimes he would stop breathing or have very long gaps in between breaths. He sustained injuries as a result of falls (although thankfully nothing major, which was a miracle in itself). He would have bad runs of seizures at night. On his worst night he had fourteen grand mal seizures in a row. We had to have oxygen and a breathing mask at home, as well as a suction machine to help him with his airway if he had a lot of secretions. He once fell down the stairs, banged his head on the wall, and stopped breathing. I did CPR, breathing for him as Beccy called the ambulance – the longest five minutes of my life.

Ambulances came not infrequently to our house in the middle of the night. We spent nights in resus in the emergency department of various hospitals, and occasionally he would be admitted for a few days at a time until the seizures had stabilized. Leaving him in hospital was difficult, but if I'm honest, it also meant that we could go home and get a night's sleep, albeit while still worrying about him and feeling guilty. I spent a lot of nights sleeping on the floor beside his bed when things were at their worst.

Over time, this took a toll on all of us as a family. Our physical and mental health suffered. We were in a permanent state of adrenaline-driven fight or flight. There was very little down time for any of us. We couldn't really expect others to be able to look after him to give us a break . . . or so we felt. I was still holding down my day job as a full-time GP, including working out-of-hours emergency shifts. I had to stop those once the nights became bad, because I would be working in an emergency department somewhere when Beccy was looking after Luke at home during another bad run of seizures. Beccy had worked in between having each of our children: Josh was born in 1999; Finn in 2002; and Zac in 2005. After that she gave up teaching to become a full-time mum.

She was still doing her best to look after the boys while managing Luke's seizures. The boys' lives were often disrupted, with any number of social occasions and family plans abandoned at the last minute, although they were very understanding and caring, and never complained.

It's said that if you put a frog in a saucepan of boiling water it will jump straight out, but if you put it in a saucepan of cold water and heat it up gradually it doesn't notice and eventually is cooked. As a family, we were the frog and the water was slowly getting hotter and hotter.

I have always thought of myself as one of life's copers. Historically, my attitude towards life's challenges could be summed up in a series of clichés, film quotations, and advertising straplines: What doesn't kill you makes you stronger; Just do it; Go big or go home; Man up; I'll get all the sleep I need when I'm dead. There's something to be said for them, in the right place at the right time. However, living by all of them every day isn't a recipe for a long, satisfying, and happy life. Real life is messy and complex. Not every situation can be dealt with satisfactorily by a one-size-fits-all mindset, uttering a mantra, gritting your teeth, and getting on with it.

I realized that in order to look after my family, I also needed to look after myself a bit better than I had been. I could feel my heart racing away in the middle of the night, waiting for and imagining the next seizure on the video monitor. Beccy shared my anxieties and it was very difficult for us to relax and enjoy each other's company. Spiritually things were difficult because we had not only Luke's seizures, but also a lot of unanswered prayers to contend with. There were a lot of conversations with God in the small hours of the morning, ranging from pleading and bargaining through to anger and despair.

Beccy and I both had big questions to ask about whether God was there, did he care, and what was the point of him? It was particularly hard to swallow our prayers not being answered, when some people at church were implying, consciously or otherwise, that maybe it was our fault that this was the case, and others were sharing at the front of church their joy at their hurty knee having got better after some prayer from their house group, or at having found the right-coloured outfit when shopping the day before. I don't blame them for sharing. They weren't trying to make us feel even worse. I did question whether some of their apparent answers to prayer really fell into the *miraculous* bracket and found myself asking God whether he might consider *not* answering all the prayers for small stuff and saving his efforts for more worthy causes.

Despite the rather no-nonsense approach I had taken to life so far, I decided it was time to invest in keeping myself healthy. I needed to build resilience and preserve my mental and physical wellbeing. I will go into details of each step I took later, but to cut a long story short, over the next couple of years I learnt more and more about the key areas that can determine our wellbeing, and started to apply this to my own life. This included mindfulness or meditation, becoming more physically active in my everyday life, making some changes to what I ate, and the quantity and quality of sleep that I was getting. Although I'm still very much a work in progress – just ask my long-suffering wife – I have seen real improvements in my own wellbeing as a result of this. More interestingly, my development of a lifestyle-medicine practice has spilled over positively into the rest of my life. It affects how I consult with patients, my relationships with my family and friends (some of whom have also made changes in their own lives), how I engage with the church and wider faith community, and the way I think about how we fund and provide healthcare to our population.

Going through this process has been life-changing. I've had my road-to-Damascus experience. The scales have been removed from my eyes. Like Neo in *The Matrix*, I've taken the red pill and now there's no going back. As a society we have lost touch with that it truly means to feel well physically, spiritually, and mentally. We have made an increasingly toxic world for ourselves that ignores what it is to be human and the needs that we have. It's not just that we've got lost on the journey to a meaningful and enjoyable existence; at times we seem to be running headlong, individually and collectively, in the opposite direction. This plays out in our faith communities too. You've heard the quote about being 'too heavenly minded to be any earthly use'. Well it applies to attitudes towards health and wellbeing too.

So far, so challenging and daunting. Let's flip this around. There's good news about how we can live lives that are fit for purpose, free of an artificial divide between the physical, spiritual, and mental. I want to share it. More than that, I feel it's my duty to share it. I haven't often felt God speaking directly in my life, or steering me to make a particular decision. Most of my big life choices have been made on the basis of common sense, gut instinct, and aspiration. Sometimes I have asked God what he had to say. There hasn't always been a clear answer and I may not have always listened that carefully. He's making up for it now though. I've felt compelled to bring together what I've learnt personally and professionally, to put on the page these words that you are reading right now.

I've done a lot of learning about wellbeing and what might loosely be termed 'lifestyle medicine' over the last few years. By 'a lot', I mean a truly ridiculous amount, approached with an attitude bordering on the obsessional. Hardly a day has gone by in the last five years when I haven't learnt something new, whether it's from reading a book or journal article, listening to a podcast, watching a video, attending a conference, or having a conversation with someone, and I've done a lot of reflecting and written a lot of notes. I've put my learning into practice, learnt from some of my mistakes, refined my technique, and done it all over again. The good news for you is that, as a result of my extensive wanderings down this particular rabbit hole, you don't need to do it all over again for yourself. Not unless you really want to, of course. So just in case you are busy, just in case you don't actually have all the time in the world to spend learning about this, just in case you have your own challenges in life that make it quite difficult to address these issues, I've taken everything I've learnt, distilled it down, distilled it down again, and put it together in the pages of this book.

Most of what I've got to share with you is common sense or inspired by the work of others. Some of it is from my own experience. I'm standing on the shoulders of giants here: devoted researchers with special interests, world-leading experts, and those who have led the way in developing lifestyle medicine as a speciality and have put wellbeing front and centre of many people's awareness. I've tried to give them credit and reference their work where I can.

My contribution to all of this is as a generalist. GPs are the last true *general* physicians. Everyone else in the medical profession is a specialist or an '–ologist', as I like to describe them. As generalists we know a little bit about a lot of things, unlike specialists who know a lot about vanishingly little. We bring our understanding together every day in our job, fusing evidence and clinical skill with pragmatism and a knowledge of the people who are our patients.

In this book I'm adding another layer to integrate all of this with faith or spirituality. This is because I believe that for us to feel truly well, to fulfil our potential and live satisfying and meaningful lives, there should not be an artificial divide between physical and mental and spiritual wellbeing. My personal experience is in a Christian context, but the principles here are broad and may be applicable whatever faith or belief system you adhere to. You may not identify with any particular belief system. There's still plenty here for you, and if it leads you to ask questions about faith and deeper meaning and purpose in the context of life and wellbeing, then so much the better.

It may be that you do follow a particular faith, perhaps the Christian faith as I do. Don't get too comfortable. Just as we need to acknowledge our spirituality to fulfil our potential as human beings, we also need to recognize our humanity as being integral to us achieving our true spiritual potential. With this in mind, we need to talk about duality.

4. Dangerous Duality

When I was younger, I used to divide my week into the spiritual and the secular. On Sunday I would go to church in the morning, Sunday school in the afternoon, church again in the evening, and then attend a group afterwards for young adults. I also met with a small group of friends on a Tuesday evening to read the Bible and pray. Those days were my *spiritual life*; the days when I got the nourishment I needed to be inspired and supercharged, so that I could step out refreshed into the secular world for the rest of the week, armed for battle and ready for the slings and arrows that life would throw at me. Okay, I am overstating it a little, but nonetheless, this was broadly the mindset that I developed, partly because that was what I had been taught by my elders and betters.

If I'm honest, the supercharging didn't usually last more than a few hours outside of these meetings and the way that I lived my life during the week was often not discernibly different from that of my friends and colleagues who were not Christians. I had a set of beliefs, a spiritual framework, and could quote verses from the Bible about this and that, but I didn't always practise what I preached. I was living a double life, existing in a duality.

As I got older, I realized that this approach wasn't helpful and that my faith should permeate my whole life – the whole week. Monday could be just as spiritual a day as Sunday. It shouldn't matter whether I was at church, school, or work. I needed to live consistently, according to my principles. By showing rather than telling those around me, I would have the most impact on the world and live the most satisfying life. I would be more authentic and effective, less conflicted. I'm not saying I've managed this every day of my life ever since, but at least I know what I should be aiming for.

Now you may be thinking at this stage that perhaps it wasn't such a good investment to buy this book, because the author is clearly not that smart, or at least, is a lot slower on the uptake than you are. So far, so bleedin' obvious. However, over the decades since I came to this not-so-remarkable conclusion, I have noticed an even greater and more concerning duality in every single church that I have ever been part of, whether Brethren, Anglican, Methodist, Baptist, or Pentecostal. This reflects a problem in wider society, but it's at least as bad in the Church.

Dualism, or duality, can have a number of different meanings. Crudely speaking it means having two parts, often with opposite meanings, like the two sides of a coin. In psychology and metaphysics (again, I'm simplifying and generalizing), it refers to mind and body, the spiritual and the physical, being separate from each other. This is the dualism that I am referring to. What I have seen over the last few decades is a growing emphasis on the spiritual while neglecting the physical and mental. An emphasis is often placed on spiritual battles having very little, if anything, to say about everyday health-related ones. This happens more in some churches than others, but it is a consistent theme. I see church leaders offering advice on spiritual matters, while ignoring their own, sometimes very obvious, physical issues – like the person offering advice on how to take a speck of sawdust out of someone's eye without addressing the plank in their own. Sacrificing your health on the altar of serving a higher spiritual cause seems not just to be inevitable but admirable; something to be acknowledged with a rueful smile and shrug before carrying on regardless.

Health is sometimes addressed in the context of miraculous healing. I have a big problem with this. Miraculous healing, by its very definition, is mysterious and (as far as I can tell, based on the actual evidence produced to date) rare, otherwise it wouldn't be miraculous. Emphasis on this takes control away from individuals who are left dependent on an act of God, rather than understanding the root cause of their health-and-wellbeing issues, taking responsibility where appropriate, and being able to plan and take control of their destiny. In addition, there are some very bizarre (bordering on the cult-like) views on why people have health challenges in their life and why they have not been healed. This approach, at best tactless and at worst cruel, makes everything much harder for those who are faced with these challenges. Take, for example, the idea that your child's congenital disease or life-limiting illness is due to some sort of unrepented-for ancestral sin. This intellectually lazy and deeply unbiblical teaching serves no one other than the person promulgating such rubbish, so they can avoid having to answer awkward questions about why miracles don't happen on demand, and why prayers and anointing with oil didn't work. I wouldn't blame any parent whose response to the person peddling this piffle was an immediate physical rather than spiritual one. I've been there and been sorely tempted.

What I'm trying to say is that healing, or at least improved health and quality of life, is something that should, as much as possible, be within the grasp of everyone, not just a few. I would argue that curing your own diabetes by making lifestyle changes is potentially just as significant as cancer being cured by miraculous or medical means.

I firmly believe that we should not separate mind, body, and soul, or the physical and the spiritual. We are human beings, made in God's image, knitted together in our mothers' wombs, fearfully and wonderfully made, as indicated in Psalm 139: 13f. If it isn't possible to separate the trinity of Father, Son, and Holy Spirit, why would we try to fragment ourselves?

Not many people would defend a church leader turning up to preach on a Sunday morning drunk or hungover. But did you know that being sleep-deprived has a similar effect? How credible is it to counsel someone about drug addiction if the counsellor themselves is addicted to food, sex, or social media? Can we talk with a straight face about the need for spiritual discipline if we have no financial or physical discipline ourselves? My GP used to sit in his consulting room with a beer belly, nicotine-stained fingertips, and a big red nose advising his patients about living a healthy lifestyle. That's the only thing I remember about him, not any of the advice that he gave.

So how do we address this? Throughout this book I'm going to look at the determinants and key pillars of wellbeing. These are sleep, movement, food, stress and relaxation, connection and purpose. They incorporate the physical, mental, social, and spiritual. I'll summarize the evidence both of the harms of not having the right balance, as well as the considerable benefits of making positive changes to address this, and will look at what the Bible has to say about these areas. Although scripture is not a textbook or a step-by-step instruction manual, it contains plenty to point us in the right direction. We will explore principles of behavioural psychology and how we can use these to nudge ourselves towards planning and achieving changes in our lives, and the lives of those around us.

Whether you are an individual looking to make changes in your own life, a church leader wanting to lead by example and to use your team and premises in the best possible way, or a group wanting to make a difference in your community, I believe that using these principles will enable us all to become fit for purpose.

5. Sleep

Come to me, all you who are weary and burdened, and I will give you rest. (Matthew 11:28, NIV)

One of my guilty pleasures in life is the movie *Road House*, starring Patrick Swayze. It's a cheesy, late-Eighties action flick about a bouncer. Sam Elliot plays his ageing, battle-scarred mentor and drawls one of my favourite lines in the film: 'I'll get all the sleep I need when I'm dead.' I lived by this for most of my adult life. I chose it as the motto for my Xbox live-gaming avatar, which probably tells you quite a lot in itself about my historically masochistic approach to this subject. We've all heard about famous people who allegedly slept very little and achieved greatness. You may know people who claim they only need a few hours a night to function perfectly well. You may be one of them. It is true, to some degree, that we are all different and may have different requirements when it comes to sleep. People may describe themselves as *larks* or *owls*, by which they mean they feel they are at their best first thing in the morning or last thing at night, and set their clocks and working patterns accordingly. However, it's only fair that I take this opportunity to give you a few facts and dispel a few myths.

Before we get into details, it's important to acknowledge that there are many factors that affect our sleep. Some may be obviously within our control, such as our 'sleep hygiene', by which I mean our routine and how we prepare for and give ourselves the best chance of good sleep. Some may not be within our control, or at least less obviously so: for instance, the environment in which we live and work, shift patterns, long-term physical and mental health conditions, and other life circumstances. The point of this chapter is not to send you into a panic and make you feel even more anxious and less likely to sleep as a result! It is to give you some information, to challenge you to make changes where you can and to offer some pragmatic tips from which you might pick and choose. Everyone, whatever their circumstances, can benefit from improved sleep.

You are designed to sleep

As a species we spend about a third of our entire lives in an unconscious, vulnerable state. This is either a huge mistake on the part of our creator and the evolutionary process, or absolutely essential for our wellbeing and continued survival. Since there are about eight billion humans and counting on the planet, there's a fairly obvious conclusion to draw from this.

As the day draws on and the light begins to fade, levels of a hormone called *melatonin* begin to rise in our bodies. This is one of the signals to our brain that the time to sleep is approaching. There is also another substance called *adenosine*, levels of which rise as the day progresses, creating the pressure or desire to sleep. We've all felt it: that moment where our eyes begin to drop and we realize we've read the same line of a book or watched the same clip on Netflix at least three times. These are naturally occurring processes in your body over which you have no conscious control. They are there for a reason. We have built-in body clocks of circadian rhythm that continue to tick round roughly every twenty-four hours, no matter what our circumstances.

Unfortunately, in the 'developed' world we seem increasingly to be building lives and societal structures for ourselves that don't just ignore these truths, but are trying to test them to destruction, to our cost. In the last century, we have lost a significant proportion of our sleep, possibly up to 20 per cent or more. This has been achieved unwittingly in a number of ways, including the use of artificial light, workday length and culture, and the use of technology to keep us permanently plumbed in and turned on, twenty-four hours a day, seven days a week. We are sleepwalking into not sleeping.

What happens when you sleep?

We are learning more and more about what happens when we sleep. One important process is essentially brain cleaning. There are cells in our brain that support our nerve cells, holding them in place. They are called glial cells. It is now known that in sleep they shrink to about half their size, allowing the flow of cerebrospinal fluid around the brain (known as the 'glymphatic system'), which helps to remove debris and toxins that have accumulated during the day.

Sleep is also important for processing information, including memories and learning. There are different parts to our sleep cycle. In deeper non-dreaming NREM (non-rapid eye movement) sleep, we process what we have learnt and discard the stuff that we don't need. In the lighter, dreaming REM (rapid eye movement) sleep, we consolidate new memories and integrate information that is important for learning and creativity. The old adage about sleeping on a problem is actually true. Both Non REM and REM sleep are important, and if either is significantly disrupted it can lead to serious consequences, which we will come onto.

When we sleep our breathing slows, our blood pressure drops, and our muscles relax. Blood flow increases to the muscles, and tissue growth and repair occurs. Hormones (such as growth hormone) are released and energy levels are restored. Sleep is fundamental to our wellbeing. It's the best gift we can give to ourselves and others. I've seen people reverse their diabetes, lose weight, and come off their blood-pressure medication as a result of just sleeping better.

How much sleep do you need?

The average amount of time that most adults need is seven to eight hours a night; children and teenagers slightly more. Bear in mind that some people fall asleep more quickly and sleep more deeply than others, so this means setting aside somewhere between seven and a half to nine hours of sleep time to achieve this. In his excellent book *Why We Sleep*, Professor Matthew Walker recommends you ask yourself whether you feel refreshed by your sleep when you wake up and whether you wake up before your alarm.[1] If the answer to both questions is 'yes', you're getting enough sleep. If not, you aren't. There are a very small number of us who genuinely don't need much sleep (probably less than one per cent of the population), who can get by with just a few hours a night. But just as most people think they are better-than-average drivers (clearly impossible, statistically speaking), most people who think they are special cases are in fact wrong. If you want to look into this in a little more detail, you could start with the SATED sleep questionnaire, which looks at your satisfaction, alertness, timing, efficiency, and duration of sleep and produces a score from 0 to 10, with 10 being very good sleep.[2]

What happens when you don't sleep enough?

There is solid evidence of the consequences of chronic sleep deprivation.[3] It increases the risks of dementia, heart disease, stroke, raised blood pressure, diabetes, cancer, inflammatory conditions, and mental illness . . . among others. The full list is a lot longer, but I'm sure you get the idea. Frighteningly, you don't need to deprive yourself of sleep for very long to develop health problems. Just a week of reduced sleep quantity and quality can induce changes in blood sugar consistent with diabetes and symptoms of acute mental illness, such as psychosis. Being relatively sleep-deprived every day for a week has a similar effect to not sleeping at all for an entire night. Disruption of your sleep will have consequences for your memory and higher cognitive functioning. Sleep deprivation in study subjects, after tasks involving memory, results in poor subsequent recall. Even just one night of poor sleep can result in being unable to recall facts you may have learnt in the preceding two or three days. So much for pulling an all-nighter to cram for that exam, or to put together a top-notch presentation for work!

If we stay up late and are tired, we tend to make poor decisions about what and when we eat. We feel hungry (owing to rising levels of ghrelin, a hormone which increases our appetite), and falling levels of leptin (its counterpart, which makes us feel full). As a result, we are more likely to reach for foods that are not ideal, such as highly processed convenience snacks that contain a lot of fat and sugar. In the long term this results in rising weight, blood pressure, and blood sugar. Late-night snacking on less healthy foods unfortunately results in a double whammy, because our body is not a factory and doesn't process everything we eat in exactly the same way, twenty-four hours a day. There is growing evidence to show that if we extend the period of time we eat in any given day (from first to last mouthful of food or alcoholic drink), we put on more weight and are less fit as a result than someone who eats and drinks within a shorter period.

Sleep also has an epigenetic effect. Epigenetics refers to how our genes are expressed. Although historically it was argued by many that genetics are *destiny* and that nature trumps nurture every time, this is thought increasingly not to be the case. Our environment and the choices that we make may well significantly influence how the genes that we have are expressed, and whether we are more or less likely to end up with problems such as heart disease, inflammatory and autoimmune conditions, mental health problems, dementia, and even cancer. Two people with an identical genetic make-up can end up with very different states of health depending on how their gene expression has been influenced. Sleep deprivation results in more turning on of inflammatory genes and the dampening down of stabilizing ones.

You can exist in a state of chronic sleep deprivation. Many of us do. You may well be considered personally and professionally successful. Just so we're clear: this is probably *despite* your lack of sleep, not because of it. You may think you're functioning fully, but there's plenty of evidence demonstrating the effects of sleep deprivation in areas such as memory, learning, driving, weight, decision-making, and personal interactions. Just like a drunk or hungover person who thinks they're fit to drive, chair a meeting, or make a big life decision, the sleep-deprived person may well have no insight into how their performance is impaired. Being sleep-deprived therefore also affects your social interactions, whether personal or professional. It may result in damage to your relationships and even limit your career prospects, without you being aware of any of this.

I often see patients with significant undiagnosed conditions, who are not aware of the impact on their wellbeing. A good example of such a condition is atrial fibrillation, in which a person's heart beats irregularly and often too fast. This may result in symptoms such as tiredness, dizziness, and shortness of breath. I once saw an older lady whose irregular pulse was picked up during a routine nursing appointment. Once she was started on medication to slow her heart rate down, she was amazed at how much better she felt and realized that she had been compensating for her tiredness and breathlessness (which she assumed was due to old age), by gradually doing less and less so that the symptoms didn't trouble her as much. Sleep deprivation has a similar effect.

The first time I gave myself the gift of seven to eight hours sleep every night for a week, I felt like a different person. I realized I had only been operating at 75–80 per cent capacity in terms of my physical and cognitive functioning, but had convinced myself that this was normal. I think this may be a particular problem for people that we might describe as 'high achievers'. If they are already fortunate enough to have the genetic, physical, emotional, educational, social, and environmental advantages that usually lead to good cognitive function and wellbeing, then they may well be operating from a higher baseline than others, which disguises the fact that they are actually impaired and operating at less than their full potential capacity. During any given episode of *The Apprentice*, I'm the first person to shout at the television, 'You can't give 110 per cent!' But just think about what the impact would be of finding the extra 20 per cent that you hadn't realized you were missing out on.

The myth of larks and owls

The idea that some people function at their best late at night rather than early in the morning, and that they should tailor their sleep time accordingly, is problematic. Although it's true that there are differences between individuals, and that these may be partially genetically determined, it's nowhere near as binary as the concept of larks and owls. We may all be at different points along a scale, but the differences are relatively minor for most of us. A person may describe themselves as a 'lark' or an 'owl' as a consequence of the choices they have made, consciously or unconsciously, for lifestyle or work-related reasons, rather than because of any innate characteristics they possess. We might do it to justify how we live our lives and to make ourselves feel better by blaming it upon something beyond our control. Before you swallow this concept whole, ask yourself the question: Is it just possible that someone who has got into the habit of staying up late is tired when they wake up in the morning and so don't feel at their best? What makes more sense for these people: to respond by shrugging and fatalistically labelling themselves as an owl? Or to consider whether they might need more sleep, with all the benefits that come with this?

I found this in my own life. It turns out that I do need a bit less sleep than some of my friends and family (about six and half hours in my case), but now instead of trying to be an owl and work late, I go to bed a bit earlier and have discovered that I'm actually a lark! I get up early most mornings now and enjoy having time to myself before the rest of the world is up. I can go for a walk, get some work done, and have time to think and pray.

It is well recognized that sleep patterns do change throughout life and that the sleep/wake cycle in adolescence is different from that in later adulthood. Much as I hate to admit it as a parent, there may be something of a scientific basis to support your teenager being a less-than-reasonable human being first thing in the morning. Most teenagers would benefit from a later start to the day. There are a small number of schools that have acknowledged this reality by shifting the school day back, starting lessons later in the morning. In reality, for most of us this is not yet an option. We do have some control over our circumstances and the decisions that we make though. This might include what bedtimes we set for ourselves and our children, and what time we start our working and school days.

If your child struggles to get up in the morning, maybe going to bed at midnight having spent hours on their mobile phone and then getting up at 6 a.m. for a paper round is not in their best interests.

What can we learn about sleep from the Bible?

Jesus led by example.

On one occasion he'd had what might be considered a busy day. I moan about a twelve-hour day, challenging work, and patients who don't always appreciate me. Jesus, however, had been driving out demons and healing the sick. That's pretty hardcore. He was surrounded by crowds clamouring all day for his attention. He was tired. He gave instructions to his disciples to cross to the other side of the lake in their boat. As they were doing this, a furious storm came up. Waves were not just pounding the boat but pouring over it. Where was Jesus? Was he running around, leaping into action, bailing out water? No, he was asleep in the hold. He knew what his body needed and was prepared to prioritize it.

You need just the right amount of sleep.

> How long will you lie there, O sluggard? When will you arise from your sleep? (Proverbs 6: 9, ESV)

The Bible does refer to sleeping too much. There is a scientific basis to this. If you plot a population-wide graph with the number of hours' sleep along the horizontal axis and mortality (death from all causes) along the vertical axis, you get a U-shaped curve.[4] This suggests that, just like any other medicine, sleep should be taken in the right dose and that you can have too much of an apparently good thing.

Not every night's sleep will be perfect

Of course, there will be times in your life when it may not be possible to get enough sleep. Occasionally it might be right to sacrifice sleep for a higher purpose. The Bible records Jesus staying up all night to pray (Luke 6:12). I remember at university the Christian Union once organized a week of continuous prayer and people signed up for shifts in the middle of the night. You might be taking part in an endurance event to raise money or awareness.

Life isn't perfect and there will be times when we don't get the sleep we need. We may not be organized enough and suddenly a major deadline looms. We may be going through a bereavement or a crisis of some sort, or might have a health condition which interferes with our sleep, whether physical or mental in origin.

I'm not stating glibly that we should all enjoy perfect sleep all the time, and that if you aren't enjoying perfect sleep it's all your fault, regardless of the reasons for it. However, my experience as a doctor, parent, and human being is that most of us have more control than we think over how well we sleep, and that it is always possible to improve the quantity or the quality of our sleep to some degree. Doing so may well lead to either preventing or improving some long-term conditions. This leads nicely onto the last part of this chapter: my tips for enjoying better sleep.

What is your sleep culture?

So far, we have focused on the individual. We need to consider the bigger picture. It's great for you and me to try our best to sleep well, but if we are part of a culture that either isn't mindful of the importance of sleep, or promotes rules of life that are destructive, we have a bigger problem than just our individual wellbeing. So now I'm asking questions of, and putting out a challenge to, churches, other faith-based organizations, and the wider community. You may be a leader in this setting. Are you leading by example and getting the sleep you need? Do you practise what you preach?

You probably wouldn't consider it acceptable to preach or drive if drunk or hungover, but do you do it when you are tired, the morning after a late-night meeting, or a box-set binge? I realized there were certain days of the week when my ability to perform and contribute was significantly impaired because I had chosen to sleep less the night before. It was pointed out to me in an appraisal a few years ago that I often looked tired and fell asleep in meetings. I was actually asked if everything at home was okay, because the person conducting the appraisal knew about my family history.

I couldn't blame it on stress because my son was living in a wonderful place, receiving fantastic care, and we were no longer on call 24/7. It was my choice; the result of years of bad habits. I wasn't giving my best. In fact, I was really cheating those that I was meant to be serving by choosing to live my life like this. I hadn't realized any of these things. As a result of the appraisal I took stock and made some changes to my habits so that I got more sleep, particularly the day before long meetings. I no longer have to fight to stay awake (usually!) and contribute more as a result.

How are you looking after and encouraging those that work with you and for you? Are work expectations manageable and fair? Are you 'always on', and do you expect others to be? Does your culture encourage an appropriate work–life balance? When you have an appraisal or mentoring session with a member of your team, do you cover wellbeing as well as performance, and do you include sleep in this? If the church is putting on a youth event, such as a weekend away, do you take this into account in your planning? I have fond memories of many a sleep-deprived weekend away from home, with my friends and youth-group leaders. I'm not suggesting that we take the fun out by no longer having midnight walks and pillow fights. It might be worth thinking about a realistic starting time for the next day's events after a late night, so that those taking part can get more out of them, and put more in. Perhaps the activity after lunch on such a day could be something more physically active and outdoor-based, with plenty of light exposure, as opposed to a sedentary and indoor one which is likely to result in a significant number of the group struggling to concentrate and drifting off to sleep.

My prescription for enjoying better quality and quantity of sleep

For individuals

1. Get up and go to bed at roughly the same time every day

Avoid trying to compensate for poor sleep during the week by having lie-ins at the weekend. A good rhythm is best for your body.

2. Get plenty of fresh air, light exposure, and exercise during the day

Morning is the ideal time of day for most of us. It regulates our body clock and helps us get to sleep more easily.

3. Avoid caffeine after midday

Bear in mind that even 'decaf' drinks can still have up to a quarter of the amount of caffeine as fully caffeinated drinks. If you're cutting back on tea and coffee, make sure you keep up your fluids during the day, particularly in the afternoons, as this increases the volume of fluid circulating throughout your body, which is important for cooling your core temperature at night and so helps sleep.

4. Reduce or cut out alcohol in the evenings

Alcohol is a sedative, but not a restorative. It leads to poor-quality and disturbed sleep. If you are going to have a late night, try not to combine it with drinking significant amounts of alcohol. One unit of alcohol will cost you about an hour's sleep. The same advice applies to sleeping tablets. They have their place very occasionally in acutely stressful circumstances, for a night or two. Overall, medical studies have shown that sleeping tablets do not result in consistently better sleep for most people. They are also addictive and may have unwanted side effects.

5. Avoid too much napping during the day

This is particularly important as you get older, since sleep quality tends to reduce with age.

6. Avoid blue light in the evenings for at least an hour or two before bedtime

This lowers your melatonin levels and makes it harder to sleep. You can cheat by putting on night-mode settings on your devices or wearing glasses which filter out certain frequencies of light, but it's much better to cut it out altogether, because it also encourages you to disengage from work and get into the right frame of mind for relaxation and sleep. It might also encourage you to spend more time with those in your real social network, as opposed to the virtual one.

7. Try a warm bath before bedtime

Light some candles, put on some music. Don't take your phone into the bath with you.

8. Don't take your phone or other devices to bed

Before you protest that you use your phone as an alarm clock, may I suggest that you buy an actual alarm clock? Preferably with a red LED display rather than a blue or white one.

9. Keep your room cool and dark

We generally sleep better at lower temperatures.

10. Mindfulness exercises can be helpful

These are particularly helpful if you find that your thoughts are whirring away at the end of the day. They are good for relaxation generally and once you have developed the practice, you can use them to help you go to sleep. I will cover mindfulness in more detail later on.

If you think you are one of those people who doesn't need much sleep, just humour me. Give yourself a trial of eight hours sleep a night for a week to see what difference it makes. The worst-case scenario is that you get a little more sleep. The best-case scenario may result in you transforming your life. If you're not sure how well you are sleeping and would like more information about the quantity and quality of your sleep (other than just listening to your own body, of course), then consider using technology to help you track this. There are plenty of quantifiable *self*-gadgets out there that you can wear, such as a Fitbit or an Apple Watch, that will give you some reasonably helpful information . . . just as long as wearing them doesn't disturb your sleep or involve you staring at a screen late at night to interpret the data!

For organizations and leaders

1. Lead by personal example

You need to be authentic. As they say in the safety demonstrations each time you fly, put on your own oxygen mask before helping others.

2. Set the sleep culture

If you are an employer, think about the job specifications and working requirements of those you are responsible for. Are they reasonable? Are you encouraging the right attitude to work, and particularly to a work–life balance? A well-slept team member is a more productive one, who will have better relationships with others, make fewer mistakes, and enjoy their work more. If you are the boss, don't send emails late at night. If you really can't help yourself, consider doing what a colleague of mine does: he puts a disclaimer along with his standard email signature which explains that although he may send emails in the early hours of the morning, he doesn't expect others to respond to them at the same time.

3. Emphasize sleep as a spiritual as well as a physical discipline

This is crucial in your position as a leader. Remember to cover this when appraising, mentoring, and teaching.

4. Think about the timing of meetings

The graveyard shift at around 2–3 p.m. is when we are most likely to experience a dip. Tailor the day accordingly and make that time more physically active and stimulating if you can. It may not be the best time for people to take in a lot of information and make important decisions. You could schedule in a walking meeting or any other physical activity that people might enjoy.

5. Make sleep a part of your preparations

If you and your organization have got a big day or weekend ahead, prepare for it. Just as you would make sure you had your notes or materials available, and would have practised a speech or presentation beforehand, give some thought to how much sleep you need and make it a part of your preparation. Be consistent over a few days. One night's good sleep after a few nights' poor sleep is not enough to make up the deficit. If you want to able to recall information you have been learning, if you need to connect and interact well with others, and make good decisions, if it's your responsibility to lead and teach people under your care, then the best preparation you can make for all of this is simply to get a good night's sleep.

Notes

1. Professor Matthew Walker, *Why We Sleep: Unlocking the Power of Sleep and Dreams* (New York: Scribner, Simon & Schuster, 2017).

2. The SATED Test (University of Pittsburgh, 2013). Available at: https:// livinglifebetter.uk.

3. S. Banks and D.F. Dinges, 'Behavioral and Physiological Consequences of Sleep Restriction', *Journal of Clinical Sleep Medicine*, 3: 5 (2007), 519–528.

4. J.E. Ferrie, M.J. Shipley, F.P. Cappuccio, et al. 'A Prospective Study of Change in Sleep Duration: Associations with Mortality in the Whitehall II Cohort', *Sleep*, 30: 12 (2007),1659–1666.

6. Food

So whether you eat or drink or whatever you do, do it all for the glory of God. (1 Corinthians 10: 31, ESV)

Food is fundamental. Food isn't just fuel. Food is medicine that heals us. Food is information, sending signals to our bodies as it is consumed and broken down into its basic components. Eating well can boost our immune system, improve the control of long-term conditions, reduce the risk of cancer occurring and recurring, and even prolong our lives. It's a bountiful gift, particularly in the developed world, where most of us live in relative affluence and can afford pretty much anything that we want, whether we pick it from the field, from the supermarket shelf, or have it delivered to our door.

Like any medicine, there is a correct dose: too little or too much is bad for us. In my younger days, I used to say to my patients that there was no point in writing my own book about eating well because I was unlikely to earn a living from selling a single piece of paper on which was written in bold the words, 'Eat less, move more'. Now I know better. If it really was that easy, there would be two consequences: firstly, no one would be overweight in the first place; and secondly, there would therefore be no diet books. No demand, no supply. However, a quick look on the High Street will reveal that lots of people are overweight (the majority of British and American adults, in fact). If you then look online, you will also see that 20–25 per cent of the bestselling health books on Amazon are diet-related. So, if it is that simple and easy then we should all be getting it right. Since we're clearly not getting it right (and by 'we' I mean the entire developed world, and now also quite a lot of the developing world), what has gone wrong?

Our toxic food environment

You will notice a recurrent theme here. The biggest determinant of how we behave, and the result of this behaviour, is not intelligence or moral fibre, but the environment in which we have been raised, live, and work. Just as we seem to have created an environment that is the opposite of what we need as human beings when it comes to sleep and movement, so it is with food. Well, at least we're consistent!

Once upon a time, long ago, we were hunter-gatherers. The clue as to how we got our food is in the title. It was, in some ways, a precarious existence. As a hunter-gatherer you couldn't guarantee where your next meal was coming from, but overall, the system suited us pretty well as a species. Then at some point around 10,000 years ago many societies decided to stay more in one place and focus on cultivating a narrower range of animals and plants. This could be termed loosely as 'the agricultural revolution'. It offered the promise of convenience and availability. With the benefit of hindsight this may not have been such a good thing. In his excellent book *Sapiens* Yuval Harari writes that the essence of the agricultural revolution was: 'the ability to keep more people alive under worse conditions'.[1] As a pragmatist I'm not going to dwell on what might have been. We now live on a planet with a population that has swollen to almost eight billion people, partly as a result of this agricultural revolution and particularly owing to intensive farming. A return to being hunter-gatherers is no longer an option. Or at least, not one that humankind would take voluntarily. Whether we end up doing this involuntarily is another issue altogether and a different book.

Once upon a time, and not that long ago, we ate wholefoods. By wholefoods I mean foods in their natural state, and which had been processed or refined (mechanically or chemically) as little as possible, if at all. The produce, whether plant or animal, was usually sourced locally. We worked hard for it, with many people being employed in manual labour, and ate what was in season. It was difficult to overeat (unless you were well-off) because availability was limited.

Today we still have the option of eating wholefoods, but there are a lot of other convenient options out there, thanks to the food industry. The shelves of our supermarkets are groaning with cheap, calorie-dense, highly processed food-like substances. You will notice my use of the words 'food-like' as they shouldn't be dignified by calling them food.

Not all processed food is bad. Much of what we eat has been through some basic processing such as freezing, baking, canning, pasteurization, or drying. Examples would include bread, milk, cheese, and canned goods. There's nothing wrong with this and some processes may be required to make some foods safe. However, once we start adding sugar, salt, additives, preservatives, and colourings, it's a totally different ball game. Examples of highly processed foods include soft drinks, ready meals, crisps, sweets and chocolates, sweetened breakfast cereals (which is almost all of them, by the way), and packaged soups.

I've heard it said that we should consider food highly processed if there are more than five ingredients in it. I think this is possibly a little harsh or simplistic, as those five ingredients could all be individual wholefoods. My rule of thumb is that if you have difficulty pronouncing the names of the ingredients and they sound more like a list of answers to a chemistry test than a meal, then you should put down the brightly coloured package, with all its claims about being healthy and low-fat, and containing however many of your five a day, and move to a different aisle – or a different shop.

The problem is not just that such food exists, thanks to our friends in the food industry (or 'Big Food' as many now refer these organizations, similar to Big Pharma and Big Tobacco), but how our environmental defaults have become set to increase the likelihood of us making poor decisions and ending up eating these toxic and damaging food-like substances, instead of nourishing, healing real food. A lot of thought, time, and money has gone into ensuring that we buy into their products and develop the required mindset. In this respect there is no difference between those companies that supply us with what we eat and drink and those that supply us with tobacco, gambling, and social media content.

The products are accessible, affordable, addictive, and heavily advertised. Consider the proliferation of fast-food shops near to, or even inside schools and hospitals, the two-for-the-price-of-one offers in the supermarket, prime-time advertising campaigns on TV, and junk-food manufacturers sponsoring the Olympics without even a trace of irony. Consider also the many millions of pounds spent by the food industry on lobbying the Government with the goal of preventing or delaying the introduction of the traffic-light food-labelling system on the front of packages. It is still not mandatory in the EU. About a third of products in the UK still do not have the red, yellow, or green boxes to show whether they are high in fat, salt, sugar, saturates, and calories.

Do you think that this is coincidence? Do you think Big Food is an entirely benign entity that just wants to make the world a better place, has no skin in the game, and isn't pushing back hard against ideas which would promote healthier eating and cut into their profits? If so, then while I am stripping the scales from your eyes, we also need to talk about the Tooth Fairy and the Easter Bunny.

I'm not going to rant any further about the food industry as I think I've given you a flavour (pun intended) of the problem when it comes to our food environment. If you would like to dig a bit deeper, I would recommend Mark Hyman's book, *Food: WTF should I eat now?*[2] and Michael Greger's *How Not to Die.*[3]

Sow the wind, reap the whirlwind

Let's look at the consequences of these environmental defaults and how our relationship with food has changed over time. The proof is literally in the pudding and we can measure this by measuring our weight and our waistlines.

According to the World Health Organization in a 2016 global report, 63.7% per cent of adults in the UK were overweight and 27.8 per cent were obese.[4] Not content with being the Fat Man of Europe, the UK appears hell-bent on catching up with the United States – where the figures are even worse at 67.9 per cent and 36.2 per cent, respectively – having failed to grasp the concept that bigger is not always better.

This presents us with many problems, one of which is the concept of a normal weight. Body Mass Index is a ratio of height to weight; specifically, your weight in kilograms divided by the square of your height in metres. Crudely, a person's BMI is defined as underweight if less than 20, with normal weight in the range of 20–25, overweight if 25–30, and obese if over 30. This is based on historical data collected for large populations over time. However, if the majority of the population in the developed world (and increasingly parts of the developing world) have a raised BMI and are considered overweight or obese, we have to ask ourselves the question of what is 'normal'.

Behavioural science tells us that one of the key factors determining our behaviour is whether we feel it is within the range of normal, the accepted default. Once upon a time, being significantly overweight or obese would not have been considered normal and therefore would have created discomfort within someone's mind and been a potential motivator for change. The risk we face now is that if we are overweight, we may compare ourselves to those around us and decide that there's no need to change because everyone else looks and feels the same. This leads to the supersizing of society, whether it's the clothes we buy or the size of the portions we consume, which in turn leads to the problem getting worse, in a vicious circle.

If the only consequences of being overweight or obese were requiring larger clothes and being the butt of unkind jokes, you could argue it wouldn't be that big a deal (although I appreciate it is for some). Unfortunately, the consequences are much more serious. Obesity is a risk factor for various diseases you can literally live without, including raised blood pressure, diabetes, heart disease, and stroke. According to the Global Burden of Disease study published in *The Lancet* in 2017, 8 per cent of global deaths are due to obesity, resulting in 4.7 million people dying prematurely in 2017.[5] This is roughly four times as many as those that die in road accidents, and five times the number of those dying from HIV. In the USA, this was over 400,000 deaths and, in the UK, over 56,000. To put this in perspective, this is more than eighty times the premature death rate from violent crime in the UK for the same year, according to the Office for National Statistics.[6] The tragic death of a young person from stabbing makes the front page of every newspaper and is met with much hand-wringing and cries for action, including changes to the law. But do we get eighty times as worked up about the tragedy of premature deaths caused ultimately by obesity? Do they result in eighty times as much action? I think we all know the answer.

Welcome to the Diet Wars

If we are all in agreement that our relationship with food is an unhealthy one, not least because of the toxic culture that we are brought up in, then we should be able to agree how to fix it, right? Aside from the big issues about how food should be grown, the impact on the planet, and the necessary politics rules and regulations around all of this, there must be a simple diet that we could all stick to. I mean, how complicated can it be? Quite complicated, as it turns out. If you want to get a taste of this, just look at how this is handled in the gladiatorial online arena of social-media and internet forums. Never have so many people gathered in such large numbers to blow so much hot air. To make such an unholy mess, use the following recipe:

- Take an uncertain, changing, and often poor-quality evidence base.

- Add vested financial, professional, and personal interests.

- Season with multiple platforms for people to express their views, often in rude and adversarial ways.

- Garnish with the idea that *I'm right* and so *you* must be wrong.

- Mix it all together and *voilà* – complete and utter chaos and confusion.

If you ask Wikipedia for a list of different diets you will see sections for belief-based diets, calorie-controlled diets, crash diets, detox diets, medical diets, vegetarian diets, and 'fad' diets. Fad diets are not easy to define. They usually come briefly and inexplicably into fashion (like leg warmers and deely boppers in the 1980s), promise big results in very little time, and focus on a very narrow range of foods, without worrying too much about sustainability or long-term health consequences.

Staying with the fashion analogy, some will be quickly and rightly derided and discarded, whereas others will endure and enter into the mainstream. I'm not going to list them all here and take up your time considering their merits. This isn't a diet book and I don't have my own customized and patented version to present. Instead, I am going to give you some principles to consider that will hopefully enable you to steer your way through all of this, providing you with some light rather than more heat and noise. Here, for your consideration, are my principles of eating well.

1. *The best diets are not diets*

For many of us the word 'diet' is associated with denying ourselves something that we like, usually with the end goal being weight loss. It's sacrifice, self-flagellation, a penance for having overindulged. It usually suggests a short-term approach, a fast fix, after which we can revert to whatever we like. A colleague of mine has been intermittently on one sort of diet or another for as long as I have known them. They really enjoy their food and drink until they get to the point where they decide they need to lose weight. Then for a week or two the rest of us guess what sort of diet they are adopting this time from the contents of their lunchbox. The Cabbage and Zero-calorie Noodle Diets both looked particularly unappetizing. The results? Rapid weight loss in the short term, gaining weight again afterwards – rinse and repeat. Classic yo-yo dieting.

This is where we get it wrong. The word 'diet' actually comes from the Greek word *'diaita'*, which means 'way of life'. A diet should be a way of eating, even a whole way of living, which is not just tolerable but enjoyable, and so sustainable as a result. It may help not even to label it as a *diet*. I have some sympathy with people who specifically want to crash diet to get into that swimming costume, dinner jacket, or wedding dress, but a healthy diet is not just for after Christmas and New Year – it's for life.

2. *Diets should be simple and affordable*

You should be able to explain your approach to eating in a sentence. The principles should be easy to grasp. If you have to refer to your notes, read a manual, or sign up to a course on YouTube, someone somewhere is overcomplicating matters, usually for money. Don't waste your time. You are unlikely to stick with any behaviour that isn't easy and simple. They should also not be expensive. It's fine in the short term to have someone turn up to your house to cook an organic meal every day, but not affordable for most of us, and not practical, in the long term. People need to be able to buy affordable food and prepare it themselves. If you want some pampering, go to a health spa for the weekend. It'll work out cheaper in the long run.

3. *Diets should be balanced*

Some people treat diets like religions. I recommend you don't do this, partly to avoid sounding preachy, and partly to avoid the pain that comes with splitting and the inter-faction fighting that will inevitably occur on the social media platform of your choice. If, however we are sticking with the religion analogy, it's definitely best to avoid extremism as this is likely to end badly. For that reason, a red flag for me is any diet which permanently excludes particular food groups. To be clear, I'm quite happy for manufactured food-like substances to be minimized or excluded, just not whole food groups. There may be medical reasons for this of course, such as having coeliac disease or a food allergy. However, those advocating extremes, such as the carnivore or vegan diet are, in my opinion, unwise.

Any diet which leaves you nutritionally deficient and having to artificially supplement – or face the increased risks of certain diseases as a result of malnutrition – is of course a personal choice and may be driven by strongly held, even admirable beliefs. It isn't natural, however, and therefore will be more complicated to sustain. There are two main flavours of food extremists, whether online or in real life: arrogant and aggressive; or smug and self-righteous. Okay, sometimes both. Some post pictures of plates of raw meat, eggs, and their six packs while deriding others as misguided, pasty-faced do-gooders. In return, the latter post pictures of home-grown, hand-woven vegetables/clothing (delete as applicable), while deriding others as eco-destroying meatheads. The truth lies somewhere in between. Everything in moderation. As strap lines go, it's not sexy or controversial and you can't really rant about it, but it's true.

4. Diets should be intentional and flexible

None of us are perfect. I've just said that everything should be taken in moderation. That includes moderation. I know that there isn't much evidence for the benefits of alcohol. Not really. I'd like to claim there is and I find myself clinging to the occasional news article that springs up in defence of a glass or two of red wine every day, despite the fact that I prefer beer. Every Friday, come what may, my fellow GPs and I gather upstairs in the staffroom at our surgery for our weekly debrief. The first question I ask any of them on a Friday morning is whether they will be attending. We even have a WhatsApp group set up specifically for this event. It's a very important meeting. At the end of the day, to celebrate surviving the week and the fact that we are all still standing, we gather together in this upper room. Instead of breaking bread and drinking wine, we share packets of crisps and nuts, washed down with a beer or a gin and tonic. We all agree that it's the best part of our working week.

Most Sunday afternoons I take my dog Prince for a walk. Or more correctly, he takes me for a walk to our local pub, the Plough. He has been well trained, to the extent that when he once got lost mid-walk as a puppy, I found him sitting outside the pub. I will order a pint for me (he can't do this yet but I'm working on it), some crisps for us to share, and we sit in the beer garden as I phone my parents for our weekly catch-up.

On each of these occasions I am making a mindful decision to eat or drink something which is not 'good for me'. Except that it is . . . just not from a nutritional perspective. The examples I have given are rituals around connecting with others, enjoying nature, and being physically active. We don't all live perfect lives. Our diets will be no exception. Eating well seven days a week is fantastic. Giving yourself the weekend off is still okay. Even eating well just a couple of days each week, or one meal a day, is better than not doing it at all. You will tend to find the more you do it, the better you feel, so the more you will want to do it.

5. Eat food, not too much, mostly plants

Michael Pollan, a *New York Times* journalist, summed up everything he had learnt about food in the seven words highlighted above, and since I can't do better, I will adopt his principle, make it my fifth principle for eating well, and expand a little on it.[7]

Eat food.

By this I mean eat real food, as close to its natural state as possible. Minimally processed, if at all. Remember there is a difference between food and food-like substances. Examples of real food include vegetables, fruit, whole grains (e.g. wholemeal bread and pasta, brown rice, barley, oats, quinoa), legumes (e.g. beans, peas, lentils), seeds, and nuts. A wholefoods diet is not the same as a vegetarian diet. It may include some minimally processed animal products in moderation, such as fish, meat, eggs, and dairy. To quote Michael Pollan again: 'If it came from a plant, eat it. If it was made in a plant, don't'.

Not too much.

Although I am not a fan of calorie-counting and try to dissuade my patients from doing this, there is some basic maths here that needs to be acknowledged. In the UK, the recommended maximum daily calorie intake (based on the number of calories that are consumed each day simply by being alive) is 2,500 for men and 2,000 for women. If you eat and drink more calories than you use in the activities of daily life, you will gain weight: a simple, undeniable truth. It is uttered frequently, loudly, publicly, and sometimes unkindly by people – mostly those who have never struggled with their own weight – who assume therefore that the answers to the problems caused by our relationship with food are therefore equally simple. They are absolutely right . . . while also being absolutely wrong. It's complicated. We'll get to that later.

It's not just the calories that count, it's where you get them from. The reason that I'm not a fan of the calorie-counting approach is that if you just go by the numbers, a doughnut contains the same number of calories as a bowl of broccoli. I think we all know these two are not the same. Two people can eat and drink the same number of calories each day, but the one consuming highly processed food and drink is going to experience worse health and a shorter life than the one eating real food. It's not just about body shape either. In fact, a new term has been coined to describe people who are not overweight, but have increased visceral (internal) fat as a result of making poor lifestyle choices when it comes to movement and nutrition. That term is TOFI: **T**hin on the **O**utside, **F**at on the **I**nside.

One of the keys to eating well, whatever is on your plate, is eating mindfully. In our always-on-the-go society, mealtimes can end up being just another thing on your to-do list, something to get through so that you can fuel up and power through the next thing in your diary. The result is a largely automatic process of shovelling down the food in front of us unthinkingly, until it's gone. Many of us have been raised with the idea that it is bad manners not to completely clear our plate. Unhelpful habits die hard and this can spill over even into social occasions when we are eating with friends and family. Taking time to savour your food, to chew each mouthful properly, and appreciate the taste and the texture, makes your meal more pleasurable. In addition, because you are eating more slowly, your body is more likely to get the message when you are full from the rising levels of the hormone leptin, which tells you this. Shovelling everything down as quickly as possible, on the other hand, tends to result in consuming greater quantities, but a less enjoyable experience – the worst of both worlds.

Mostly plants.

I'm an omnivore, not a vegetarian. I do not advocate veganism, at least, not without supplementation to avoid malnutrition (B12, for example). This is necessary because there are some nutrients that are only obtained in significant quantities from animal products and it simply isn't practical to get them through other natural dietary sources. That said, those of us that are fortunate enough to live in societies where meat is both available and affordable probably do, on average, eat more of it than is good for us. Quite apart from the environmental costs, there is reasonable evidence to suggest there is a cost to our health too.

You will be familiar with the headlines splashed intermittently across the front pages of our newspapers and trending on social media about sausages and bacon causing cancer . . . or not, depending on what week it is. In my opinion, the overall direction pointed by the growing body of evidence is that too much meat does very slightly increase our risk of some significant conditions, including certain types of cancer, particularly colorectal cancer. The World Cancer Research

Fund report in 2018 recommended limiting red or processed meat to 500g a week, or 70g a day.[8] Processed meat has actually been classified as carcinogenic. It's a small risk over a lifetime and one of the choices that we make along with how much sleep we get, the amount of movement in our daily lives and whether we drink alcohol or smoke. There is still controversy in this area.

My recommendation is to have at least a few meat-free days a week. When you do have meat, consider it a luxury and a side serving rather than the main bulk of the meal. Dr Mark Hyman helpfully recommends we think of it as 'condimeat'.[7] White meat, including fish, is not generally considered to increase cancer risk. The more interesting question for me is what the underlying mechanism might be for some foods to cause disease: it could be the turning on of pro-inflammatory, pro-cancerous genes and the turning off of protective ones; or perhaps the chemicals released when meat is cooked. An increasingly likely candidate is oxidative stress.

The oxidative process is an eternal battle waged throughout our bodies and is important in ageing, inflammatory disease (including cardiovascular disease), and cancer. On one side we have free radicals: unstable and highly reactive molecules, atoms, or ions that arise naturally within our own bodies, and are also produced by external factors such as X-rays, ozone, smoking, air pollution, and chemicals (including those found in ultra-processed foods). These cause damage to our cells, even the DNA inside our cells. On the other side we have antioxidants, which neutralize free radicals and protect us. Examples include vitamins C and E, alpha and beta carotene, and selenium. Like free radicals, some antioxidants are produced by our bodies and we can also get some of them from some of the foods we eat. If we have too much free-radical activity and not enough antioxidants to neutralize the free radicals, we end up with oxidative stress and damage, leading to accelerated ageing and disease processes.

Plant-based foods contain proportionately more antioxidants than meat, possibly sixty-four times as much, according to Michael Greger, in his book *How Not to Die*.[3] Examples of foods rich in antioxidants include berries (blue and red), grapes, nuts, dark green vegetables (e.g. broccoli, spinach, kale), orange vegetables (e.g. carrots, sweet potatoes, butternut squash), beans, whole grains, tea (particularly green tea), and dark chocolate. In short, your ideal plate of antioxidants should consist predominantly of a mixture of colourful vegetables and some fruit, garnished with plenty of herbs and spices (also a powerful source of antioxidants), perhaps served with a portion of fish and washed down with a cup of green tea.

I need to add a caveat here. Although this is an interesting and entirely reasonable theory, and there's really no downside to loading your plate up with vegetables, so far the evidence for improving your health with supplements remains inconclusive. In particular, there is no evidence that artificial supplementation with pills containing these antioxidant compounds has any measurable benefit. Insofar as there ever is a general consensus in the world of diet and nutrition, there seems to be one that if you are going to get your antioxidants, get them naturally from food, not from a bottle of pills.

Another reason to recommend eating a variety of different plant-based foods is because it's good for your gut microbiome.

The topic of the microbiome is a fascinating and complex one, on which many books have already been written. 'Microbiome' is the term used to describe all the microorganisms that live inside your digestive tract, and include bacteria (friendly and unfriendly), viruses, fungi, and others. The microbiome is a mysterious domain. I once heard a gut specialist compare it to the floor of the deepest parts of the ocean, in terms of the amount that we still don't know and have yet to discover. Put very simply, these organisms are considered important to our digestion and metabolism. They may influence our health directly, communicating with our brain and immune system among others. The more varied your gut microbiome, the better. Eating a limited diet of the same foods all the time, particularly if highly processed, results in reduced diversity. This can be demonstrated by analysing your poo, in case you really wanted to know.

This reduced diversity may in turn be associated with an increased risk of conditions such as obesity, inflammatory bowel disease, heart disease, and cancer. The best way to have a good variety of these bugs in your gut is to eat a good variety of plant-based foods. There are those who push the idea of dietary supplementation with friendly bacteria (we would crudely label these as probiotics), and you can buy tubs of these from health food shops. In some countries it is routine practice to take a probiotic alongside any antibiotic, to reduce the risk of unwanted side effects, such as thrush or bowel upset. There is not, as yet, any widely accepted consistent evidence of altered clinical outcomes with such supplementation, but there is plenty of research still to be done in this area.

A word about low-carb and low-fat diets

Although I have tried to keep my principles of eating well broad and simple, and declared that I have no vested interest in promoting any particular diet, I would like to take a moment to go a little deeper into one in particular that illustrates changing evidence and thinking over time, and one that I have benefited from myself — a mix of evidence-based and anecdotal-based medicine if you like.

In the middle of the last century, we came to a fork in the road with regard to our understanding of what constitutes a healthy diet and the recommendations around this. An important key figure in this was Ancel Keys, an eminent American physiologist, who had invented K-rations for the troops in the Second World War and conducted research into starvation. He was a leading proponent of the theory that saturated fat was the primary cause of heart disease. Eventually this theory received mainstream acceptance and resulted in dietary guidelines that emphasized the importance of a low-fat diet. There were dissenting voices, such as John Yudkin, a British physiologist, who believed that sugar was the real problem, as addressed in his book *Pure, White and Deadly*[9] There's nothing like a difference of opinion to cause a conflict of interests when professional reputation is at stake. Yudkin was heavily criticized by Ancel Keys for some of the methodology of his research. The food industry, very unhappy with Yudkin's message, used its considerable resources to ensure he was discredited and his message lost for decades until a resurgence of interest in this area resulted in his book being republished in 2012.

The widespread acceptance of the low-fat approach in the 1950s and 1960s was the fork-in-the-road moment, or perhaps the *fork-on-the-plate* moment. Assuming that Keys was broadly correct (he may well not have been, but we'll come to that), with hindsight, the problem is that not enough thought was given to considering what we should put on our plates instead of fat. The answer, unfortunately, in most cases was carbohydrates and highly processed food. The food industry seized upon this guidance. In the decades that have followed, we have seen an abundance of foods, particularly prepared meals, loudly labelled as being 'low-fat'. They are indeed low-fat, but unfortunately, they are also ultra-processed and usually full of sugar. Take breakfast cereal, for example. With very few exceptions, when we eat a bowl of our favourite cereal, fresh from the supermarket shelves and adorned with claims about it being low-fat, good for our hearts, and containing at least one of our five a day, we are mostly eating a bowl of sugar with absolutely zero nutritional content, usually with a spoonful or two of extra sugar on top just for good measure.

American dietary guidelines recommended the increased consumption of carbohydrates, with advice about how many helpings of grains a person should have each day. So, what has been the consequence of following these recommendations? The Carbocalypse: a carbohydrate-fuelled catastrophe. If the guidance was correct, if the right kinds of healthy food were promoted by the food industry, and if most people followed the public health advice of the time, then we would expect a reduction in overweight, obesity, diabetes, and heart disease, right? Wrong. Not only has there not been a reduction, but populations across the world, in both developed and developing countries, have seen a rocket-powered boost in the wrong direction. According to the World Health Organization, obesity has nearly tripled since 1975.

There are many environmental factors that could explain this, such as our increasingly convenient and sedentary lifestyle, but our food intake must be at least highly significant if not the primary cause.

What do I mean when I use the term carbohydrates? To keep it simple, I describe them as the *beige* foods that you put on your plate and in your mouth: bread, pasta, rice, potatoes, cakes, cereals, biscuits, crisps, and chips (or 'chips' and 'fries' as the last two would be called in the USA). The important thing to remember about all carbohydrates is that they are basically sugar with varying degrees of complexity. Eating a few slices of bread or a bowl of rice may seem a healthier choice than a chocolate bar, but they can have a similar or worse effect in terms of the rise in blood sugar you experience as a result. When your body processes carbohydrates by breaking them down into sugar, the end product is either taken up into your cells to be used for energy, stored in your muscles, or turned into fat by your liver. How ironic is it that in eating a highly processed food-like substance labelled proudly as 'low-fat' and containing things that are good for you, you are more likely to end up overweight, diabetic, and with a raised cholesterol and greater risk of cardiovascular disease?

Carbohydrates do have their place, of course. They may not contain many, if any, nutrients, but they do contain energy and you may need to load up on this if you are about to trek across a mountain range, run a marathon, or take to the sports field.

Let's be honest though – this doesn't apply to most of us, most of the time. There are also many world-class athletes who do perfectly well without significant carbohydrate intake. The ironically entitled 'NHS Eat Well Plate' has been a calamity in this respect, advocating historically that almost half of our plate should be covered in starchy foods. Fortunately, there is increasing recognition that the plate is out of date, and I advocate to my patients and clients that half their plate should be full of colourful vegetables, a quarter should be protein (fish, meat or meat substitute, eggs, beans, nuts, and seeds), and if they really want to have some carbs, they should make up no more than a quarter of the plate, and ideally, any pasta or bread or rice should be wholegrain. The value of a lower carbohydrate diet is increasingly recognized, particularly for people who have tried and failed to lose weight in the past in the conventional way, or for those who have pre-diabetes or diabetes. Organizations such as Diabetes UK officially endorse this as an option now. There is also encouraging evidence that a successful self-management programme can be delivered digitally. Dr David Unwin presented his published findings at the British Society of Lifestyle Medicine Annual Conference in 2020, demonstrating a reduction in blood-sugar levels, weight, and the need to use diabetes medication.[10] This is great news as not everyone is willing or able to attend traditional face-to-face appointments and this presents a much more accessible option. I would like to finish by stressing that I am recommending considering a *lower*-carb diet, not a *no*-carb diet. Remember my third principle of eating well – that diets should be balanced.

Now for something inflammatory

Once upon a time it was thought that coronary heart disease was caused by furred-up coronary arteries, which in turn were caused by having high levels of cholesterol. Now I'm not going to make the mistake of getting sucked into the Great Cholesterol Wars (if you'd like to read some thought-provoking writing on the matter, try Dr Malcolm Kendrick's *A Statin Nation*)[11] but it's fair to say that cholesterol is, at most, just part of the picture. Evolving evidence poses an increasing challenge to such a simplistic approach, which tends to cause great unhappiness among certain types of cardiologists, whose reason for getting up in the morning is so they can intervene dramatically in people's lives by sticking stents into their furred-up coronary arteries. It also causes equal unhappiness amongst companies operating within the health industry, particularly those that either make drugs to lower cholesterol, or make stents for the aforementioned cardiologists to use. There are some uncomfortable facts to be faced, such as people with low cholesterol levels still having heart attacks and strokes, and the treatments I have referred to (cholesterol-lowering drugs known as statins, and coronary artery stents) not actually preventing most people from dying before their time.

Yes, you did read that last line correctly.

Imagine you are one of a group of average people who is not considered to be at high risk of a heart attack, but nonetheless you are prescribed a statin to take every day for five years. I know what you're thinking: why on earth would you do that? Well, because the guidelines produced in the UK by the National Institute for Health and Care Excellence effectively mandate doctors to offer this to all men over 60 and all women over 70. Do you know what the odds are that taking this statin will prevent you having a heart attack, or a stroke? Just under 1 in 100 and 1 in 150, respectively. Or to put it another way, fewer than 1 per cent will be prevented from having a heart attack, and even fewer will be prevented from having a stroke. Despite taking a tablet every day, for five years, with blood tests, doctors' appointments, potential side effects, and drug interactions. Actually, the tablet is more likely to harm you, with a 1 in 50 (2%) chance of causing diabetes and a 1 in 10 (10%) chance of causing muscle damage. It gets worse. Even if a heart attack or stroke is prevented, do you know what the chance is that your life will be saved by taking this tablet? Zero. Zilch. *Nada.* You won't live any longer. Not so excellent after all then. If you want to find out more, take a look at this 'Statins for Heart Disease Prevention (without Prior Heart Disease)' on the actually excellent NNT.com website.[12]

I'm not going to upset cardiologists even more (some of them are my friends!) by going into the evidence around stents in great detail. I will summarize, however, by saying that they are great, life-saving things if you present to hospital having a heart attack, and a big waste of everyone's time if used routinely in people with stable heart disease who are not acutely unwell. Most people won't live a day longer with one in, and might in fact die sooner if they are unlucky enough to suffer a complication as a result of the procedure.

So, if cholesterol isn't necessarily the villain — for most of us at least — in the story of cardiovascular disease, what other causes or contributing factors might there be? And while we're at it, is there any chance that there could be an underlying, unifying process that causes not just heart disease but other long-term conditions, and maybe even cancer? It's funny you should mention this, because there is an alternative explanation, another suspect lurking in the shadows. It's not a naturally occurring chemical or a man-made toxin. It isn't so much a single thing, but more a pathway. It may be the common cause for much of what ails us. Inflammation.

There is increasing interest in and growing evidence for inflammation being the smoking gun when it comes to all sorts of maladies: heart disease, depression, diabetes, and cancer, among others. Some conditions that are inflammatory in origin have been known about for a long time, such as certain types of inflammatory arthritis, skin, or bowel disease. They can range from mild to very severe and disabling. The medical profession treats them with various types of therapy which, in one way or another, are designed to reduce inflammation. What has also been known for a while is that there is an association between an increased risk of cardiovascular disease and certain types of inflammatory disease, such as rheumatoid arthritis.

Why am I banging on about inflammation? Because understanding this as a possible mechanism for disease helps us to think about how we can adopt lifestyle measures which are anti-inflammatory. These include our sleep, our movement, our relationships, how we manage stress . . . and what we eat. Carbohydrates are *pro*-inflammatory. This can be demonstrated by measuring levels in the blood of inflammatory markers such as high-sensitivity CRP (C-reactive protein) or interleukin-6.[13] Foods with a lower glycaemic index (GI, a measure of how quickly food raises blood glucose levels) have a mild but measurable anti-inflammatory effect. Eating a lower-carbohydrate diet inevitably means eating lower GI foods. This matters because we have now come full circle back to oxidative stress, one cause for which is – yes, you've guessed it – inflammation.

How I discovered that food was medicine

I didn't know about any of this five years ago when I was diagnosed with inflammatory bowel disease (IBD). I began passing blood in my stools. I was referred urgently to a specialist who, rather than reassuring me, actually looked a bit worried and arranged for a number of other tests, including a delightful procedure known as a colonoscopy. In this day and age, the joys of technology mean that you not only get to experience the discomfort of the procedure, but also to watch the inside of your bowels (should you be so inclined) live on a TV. My bowel was inspected and samples taken and I was diagnosed with IBD.

The specialist wasn't sure which type, but it affected the lower end of my bowel. My initial reaction was a huge sense of relief that it wasn't cancer and I put my plans on hold for making the YouTube video for my kids. However, I was a little less delighted when it was explained to me that the treatment for this condition was to squirt a tube of liquid up my bottom once or twice a day, possibly forever. I asked about diet. I was told that it didn't really make much difference, so I didn't give this any thought. I got used to my new bedtime routine, which wasn't the best part of my day but was tolerable, and it kept the problem under control. From time to time I would reduce and stop the meds, either intentionally or because I forgot, and after a week or two the symptoms would recur and I would have to start treatment again.

I had been treating myself for about a year when, entirely coincidentally, I decided that I wanted to lose about half a stone in weight as, over the years, my BMI had crept up into the slightly overweight zone. I've never really had to diet, having been slim all my life, even when I was not particularly active in my early twenties. The downside to this was that I had no experience of dietary discipline and denying myself the things that I normally liked to eat and drink. The fact that I had this perception of 'dieting' in itself shows how little I understood about eating well. Eventually, after trying and failing to be strict with myself, which I rebelled against with every fibre of my being, I read about the lower-carbohydrate approach. It made sense to me. I stopped eating cereal and toast for breakfast and instead enjoyed alternatives such as eggs, fish, vegetables (even some bacon occasionally), and sometimes porridge (it's still a carb, but it has a lower glycaemic index). I had salad rather than sandwiches for lunch. I still had the odd snack, but introduced more nuts and berries into my diet. I still enjoyed a beer or two with my friends.

My wife was very supportive and happy to eat the same food, so in the evenings we cut back on the chips, potatoes, and bread and we ate more vegetables. It felt easy to do. The food was nice. I didn't feel I was denying myself. I lost half a stone, gradually, over three months. I expected this. What I didn't expect was that I would accidentally cure my IBD. As usual, I cut back on my meds to see how things went . . . and nothing happened. First, for a few weeks, then a few months, now a few years. I haven't had to take medication since I began to eat fewer carbohydrates. My tests are normal and I don't have to go to the clinic any more. It really didn't occur to me until a few months in that my change of eating habits and my condition improving might be related. I also noticed that I had more energy and was sleeping better. Not only that but my lipid profile improved despite not pursuing a 'low-fat' diet. My total cholesterol went down, and the proportion of it that was considered protective (the HDL or high-density lipoprotein bit) went up. Irrespective of whether all of this was down purely to me changing what food I ate or whether it simply assisted with the treatment I was taking, I'm pretty happy with the end result. It's not a medical trial, but personal experience is undeniably powerful in shaping the way we think. Sometimes there is a place for anecdote-based medicine to complement the evidence-based stuff.

Obesity: one size doesn't fit all

So far in this chapter I have written about the rising tide of obesity, which is one consequence of the toxic, default settings in our environment, including what we now know to be decades of incorrect advice about what constitutes healthy eating. It's undeniably true that if you take in more calories than you use in the everyday activities of living, you will gain weight. If it was easy for us all to either avoid or address this, then there wouldn't be a problem, but it's clearly not that straightforward. It's important to consider our relationship with food. Obesity can be a complex and multifactorial issue.

It is generally accepted that adverse experiences in life, particularly in childhood, are associated with an increased risk of obesity and other types of disordered eating.[14] Adverse experiences in childhood might include abuse (physical, sexual, emotional, neglect), bullying, serious injury or illness, and poverty. If you have suffered such experiences, your relationship with food may well be complicated. Using food might be a mechanism you have adopted to cope with pain. If you use it to self-soothe then denying yourself, as required by conventional 'dieting', is probably not going to work. Telling someone who is obese that they just need to lose weight is like telling someone in pain that they just need to take painkillers. It doesn't address the root cause.

As a society we are both overfed and undernourished, physically ,emotionally, and spiritually. A few decades ago, it was more likely, if you were obese as a child or young adult, that adverse life experiences were the issue. Nowadays, we are faced with a double tragedy. The first tragedy is that because of the toxicity of our environment and default settings, many people who have never suffered any significant adverse life experience are overweight or obese. At this stage, society may no longer accept them because of their being overweight or obese, which then causes pain in itself, even if this wasn't the original reason for them being overweight to start with.

The second tragedy is that, while we rightly try to find broad, public-health-based solutions to this pandemic (such as food labelling, sugar tax, better food in schools, and measures that encourage the public to be more physically active), those who have suffered trauma in their lives are lost in the crowd, all tarred with the same brush. Looking at the emotional, psychological, and spiritual aspects of your wellbeing is the essential first step for some, before they can then go on to make successful, sustainable changes. You may need to get support to understand your pain and focus on losing the feelings of inadequacy and being unworthy of love, rather than focusing on losing weight. We need to avoid oversimplification, show kindness to ourselves and others, and remember that just as we are all different shapes and sizes, so is the solution for each one of us.

What does the Bible say about eating and drinking?

Eating and drinking is an act of worship.

> So whether you eat or drink or whatever you do, do it all for the glory of God. (1 Corinthians 10: 31, ESV)

I don't know about you, but when I think of worship, more often than not, I visualize people singing and praying. Worship isn't just confined to a church service though. Our whole lives, every minute of every day, can be an act of worship, giving glory to God. How we eat and drink is no exception. Choosing what sort of food we eat, being mindful of where it has come from and grateful for it, are all part of our relationship with God and our witness to others. By now I hope that you have got the message that I don't preach perfection. However, it is worth considering what the choices we make say about how we look after ourselves and others. This might be in terms of our own bodies and immediate health, the wellbeing of others (including those that provide us with and serve us the food we eat), and the wider environment that we all live in and share. Are your spending decisions influenced by where your food comes from and the livelihoods of those that provide it? Or by the impact on the environment of the processes that bring the food to you as its consumer? Are you grateful for the food that you eat, appreciating it and savouring the experience? Eating a meal mindfully makes it more enjoyable and because we tend to slow down when doing so, we are more likely to get the message when we are full, which means we are less likely to overeat.

Food is not clean or unclean

Everything that lives and moves about will be food for you. Just as I gave you the green plants, I now give you everything. (Genesis 9: 3, ESV)

For everything God created is good and nothing is to be rejected if it is received with thanksgiving.
(1 Timothy 4: 4, NIV)

You say 'I am allowed to do anything' – but not everything is good for you . . . I must not become a slave to anything. (1 Corinthians 6: 12, NLT)

There are parallels between the debate both in the New Testament (i.e. from the time of Jesus onwards) and the present day about what we consider 'clean' and 'unclean'. In New Testament times these were used to describe foods that were considered acceptable or unacceptable from a religious perspective, and in today's climate it's usually from a physical or environmental (and so sometimes moral) perspective. In New Testament times there was debate about whether the foods avoided traditionally, following Old Testament teaching, could now be safely consumed as they were living in an age of grace (as a result of Jesus' death and resurrection), rather than according to the law that preceded it. Now the debate is about whether the food comes from a plant or an animal, whether it has been processed, and what the environmental impact of producing it has been.

For me, the take-home message is the same: we live in a world of bountiful food supply (or at least it would be if it was shared equitably), which includes both plants and animals. It's been created by God and it's all good. After all, he said so after making it. No food is forbidden. No one can line up claiming that their dietary practice, whether vegan or carnivore, or anything in between, is the only right way. The fact that we can eat anything, however, doesn't mean that we should. We should practise moderation. We should avoid eating too narrow a range of food, thus reducing the variability of the organisms in our gut, which we now know to be a bad thing and likely to cause health problems or becoming too stuck in our ways and even addicted to particular ways of eating. Addiction is more likely to occur if we are eating a diet high in sugary, processed food. After all, it has been shown that rats find the sweetness of sugar more rewarding than cocaine.[15]

We shouldn't beat ourselves up if it doesn't go to plan

**Food will not commend us to God. We are no worse off if
we do not eat and no better off if we do.
(1 Corinthians 8: 8, KJV)**

**The temptations in your life are no different from what
others experience. And God is faithful. He will not allow
the temptation to be more than you can stand. When
you are tempted, he will show you a way out so that you
can endure. (1 Corinthians 10: 13, NIV)**

Remember that the desire to eat something 'unhealthy' is a
passing one, often born out of habit and boredom. If you have the
right strategies in place, such as a healthier alternative snack or
a distracting activity, they increase the chance you will manage
this. Although it's all well and good to have a plan, there will be
times when it doesn't quite work out, or you intentionally take a
break or make a different choice. That's okay. God doesn't value
us based on how many calories we have eaten, whether they
came from an animal or a vegetable, or how highly processed
the food was. Whatever decisions we make, whatever our
intentions are, we should still be kind to ourselves.

People need to be fed physically to grow spiritually

In the story of Jesus feeding the five thousand (Matthew 14: 13–
21), he recognized the crowd's basic human needs. People were
tired and hungry and had travelled a long way to hear him speak.
He didn't separate spiritual from physical nourishment. For us

to be in the right frame of mind, to be at our best cognitively, and to perform to the best of our ability, we need to be fed. We also need to think about those around us who find it harder to feed themselves. Nutrition is vital for learning as well as other aspects of wellbeing. The Church in the UK has an important role to play in feeding the hungry, such as providing food banks and other community initiatives. We also need to lobby those in power to make the right decisions when it comes to issues such as poverty and free meals. Of course, this is basic human decency and not solely the province of faith groups. Consider the campaign conducted by Marcus Rashford, the England and Manchester United footballer, during the Covid-19 pandemic. His single-handed campaign on social media for extending free school meals resulted in repeated Government U-turns.

It's all about relationships

> **And they devoted themselves to the apostles' teaching and the fellowship, to the breaking of bread and the prayers. (Acts 2: 42, ESV)**

> **Man shall not live by bread alone but by every word that comes from the mouth of God. (Matthew 4: 4, ESV)**

It's not just our relationship with food that counts, it's our relationship with each other and with God. Eating together was an important part of Jesus's relationship with his disciples, and it remains an important part of us enjoying fellowship with each other today, in whatever setting, faith-based or secular.

It's not just good for the body, it's good for the soul, and one of the ways that we connect with each other, whoever we are, and however different our situations and philosophies.

True satisfaction in life comes not from what we have on our plate but from a meaningful existence, which includes relationships. Our ultimate relationship is with the creator who gave all of this to us. If we get this right, everything else will flow from it, including a healthy mindset when it comes to food and eating well.

What is your food culture?

I've spent a lot of time describing the challenges of the culture we have around food in wider society. What about our culture within the Church and wider Christian community?

I have already referred to the importance of the Church in feeding the hungry, following the example of Jesus. This is a great and necessary thing. You could argue that when putting together a food box for someone who can't afford to feed themselves or their family, our first priority might not be to consider whether the food has been grown organically and sourced ethically, is of low impact environmentally and not too processed or carbohydrate-heavy. Such worries are a luxury that many don't have. Mass catering, so often a feature of the Church social calendar, may well involve feeding hundreds of people and be a significant challenge. Consideration will be given to cost and convenience. However, we should also consider that showing care for ourselves and each other doesn't stop at feeding each other. It's also about feeding each other with the right stuff. Let's remember that Jesus did pretty well catering for 5,000 with just fish and bread, without a preservative or artificial sweetener in sight.

Vital, visible leadership

When it comes to a healthy and balanced approach to life, I believe that it is the responsibility of those in leadership positions within the faith community to lead by example. Now I need to issue a disclaimer here: obesity is the result of disordered eating, the causes of which are many and complex. I have already written about the importance of showing kindness to ourselves and others. Leaders deserve as much of this as everyone else. I'm not suggesting that no one with a visible eating disorder, whether over- or underweight, should be permitted to lead, or that the induction pack for the new vicar should include an approved diet sheet. That said, the best leaders lead by example and inspire others. If there is an obvious disconnect between what they practise and what they preach, it risks undermining the message and lessening their effectiveness and ability to help others.

I once attended a service at our church where every single person leading from the front was either overweight or obese. Whether they were welcoming guests, reading the notices, preaching or leading the worship, they all had the same physical issue, and whatever the reasons behind it, it was striking. What concerned me more was that I knew that not all of these people had had this problem to the same extent when they'd first started to work at the church. It was a depressing reminder of some of the principles of behavioural psychology. They worked closely together as a team, meeting regularly throughout the week, and sometimes eating and drinking together. Without realizing it they had cultivated a team environment, led from the top, which accepted being overweight or obese as a norm, and for some this resulted in the problem either starting or getting worse in the time they were working there.

You may be feeling uncomfortable or even hurt as you read these words. You may think my comments are unfair or unkind. Some pain can be masked, hidden away internally, and never acknowledged, whereas for many people who are overweight or obese they have no choice but to wear it publicly. I'm not saying that God, whose strength is made perfect in our weakness, can't use us if we are less than perfect. When I was growing up, one of the most important and influential people in my life was a man who had dedicated himself single-mindedly to serving God. He was a force of nature, a powerful preacher who gave much of himself and expected much of others, particularly the young people that he trained up to lead and to serve. Like all of us, he had some character flaws and was also morbidly obese and suffered from heart problems as a result. This shortened his life and consequently the length of time in which he was able to do his work, but it was still powerful work.

I'm not proposing that every sermon should start with a micro workout led by piously by someone in Lycra, or that churches should replace their plates of biscuits with bowls of kale (well, not entirely – we'll get onto that). However, if the significant people in our lives don't lead by example, whether parents, doctors, bosses, or church leaders, we could consider them at the very least to be flawed if not outright hypocrites. When it comes to leading a faith community, it's okay to acknowledge you are a flawed human being, just like everyone else around you, but it's not okay to be a hypocrite. If a leader is giving out messages about self-love, acceptance, self-control, spiritual discipline, and worship, they need to acknowledge that, like the rest of us, they are a work in progress. They also need to demonstrate that progress over time in order to be authentic and credible.

My prescription for eating well

For individuals

1. *What you eat matters*

Remember: eat real food; not too much; mainly plants. Eat the rainbow, by which I mean eat lots of different-coloured fruits and vegetables. Eat antioxidants: herbs, spices, berries, beans, nuts, seeds, green tea. Don't eat highly processed food on a regular basis. Most people who are struggling to lose weight or have an existing problem like pre-diabetes or diabetes will do better eating fewer carbs. A crude but effective way of remembering how to do this is to eat less *beige* food and cover at least half your plate in colourful vegetables. If you plan your meals for the week, and have a routine required to make this possible – such as setting aside time to prepare your breakfast or lunch the evening before – you are more likely to achieve success and avoid raiding your cupboards for food-like substances when you are in a rush.

2. When you eat matters

There is growing evidence that the timing of when we eat matters. Fasting is an ancient tradition across many faiths. A more contemporary, secular term is 'time-restricted eating'. If you can restrict the interval between your first and last bite to somewhere between 8 and 12 hours, you are likely to end up leaner and fitter than if you ate exactly the same food over a longer period. Our bodies aren't factories and they don't process food in exactly the same way, twenty-four hours a day, regardless of when we eat. Try to avoid eating late.

3. How you eat matters

Unless you are in the middle of some kind of eating competition, food is not just fuel to be shovelled down mindlessly and as quickly as possible. Eating mindfully makes our meals both more enjoyable and meaningful, particularly if we can share this experience with others. There's nothing wrong with dinner in front of the TV when it's movie night, but there is also value in setting the table and setting aside time together. Savour each bite of food you eat, thinking about the flavour and texture. Chew slowly. Think about how it has come to be on your plate and take a moment to be grateful for it. Put your knife and fork down in between mouthfuls. Remember that food isn't just food. It's nourishing, healing medicine.

4. Your food environment matters

We can strike back against the default, toxic environments we find ourselves in by choosing to set up our own positive, healthier ones. If you don't fill your cupboards full of crap, you won't be able to eat it. Look at what you buy each week.

Do you need to remove some foods from your favourites list in your online shop? Buy foods that you keep within arm's reach for healthier snacks (e.g. nuts, seeds, berries, and other fruit). Set up your food environment for success, whether at work or at home, by placing the less healthy snacks that you would still like to enjoy occasionally in less convenient places (e.g. at the back of the top shelf in a cupboard), so that you have to seek them out intentionally rather than grabbing them because they are convenient. I have a packet of ginger biscuits on the top shelf of my study for when I'm writing. In fact, I'm about to enjoy one after finishing this paragraph. I love them, but I just get through fewer of them this way. Plus, it stops my kids from stealing them. Ever seen a teenager attack a biscuit tin? I've seen more frightening things, but only in shark documentaries or zombie films.

5. How you treat yourself matters

Be kind to yourself. Accept yourself for who you are. Remind yourself that you are loved and valued by God and by others. Don't define yourself by your body mass index (BMI). If you are struggling with your weight, instead of calling yourself obese, think of yourself as someone who, because of their life experience and circumstances, happens to be carrying extra weight at the moment. It's not who you are. It's not destiny. It's not out of your control. Make simple changes that are easy to sustain so you avoid setting yourself up to fail, and instead celebrate victories, however small. Ask yourself every day whether you are making choices for yourself that are founded in self-love and appreciation. When you have developed a long-term goal, use a timeline to then reverse-engineer the realistic plan that will enable you to get there. Choose to develop yourself, or achieve something, in a way you can aspire to positively rather than reacting negatively to what you are not.

For organizations

1. Don't just feed people; help them to feed themselves

If we are here to love and serve our community, then we should help to feed them. Food banks are lifelines for some, particularly in times of austerity and unemployment. They are also an unfortunate reflection of the failure of wider society and the policies of successive governments. Criticism is frequently levelled at charities that merely supply food to people in developing nations. It may be right in the heart of the moment and the heat of a crisis, but it's not the long-term answer. You will have heard one version or other of the proverb that says, 'Give a man a fish and he will eat for a day; teach him how to fish and you feed him for a lifetime.' I believe that the same principles should apply in our developed world.

For the Church to be effective it must be part of society and equally, must be part of making society a fairer place. If you're planning how to set up and run a food bank in your church, make sure you are also engaged in tackling poverty, or in teaching people how to shop and cook healthily, as well as other aspects of social prescribing. The church, both as a building and as a body of people, can be a hub for this, by bringing these services and the people that need them together. My church runs a local branch of Christians Against Poverty, a fantastic organization that helps people to become debt-free, regardless of whether they have a faith or not.

2. Set the culture

If you recognize that there are issues to address in your organization, in terms of food and weight, don't let them go. Address them sensitively and supportively. I'm not suggesting that there be a discussion about hip-to-waist ratio included in your annual appraisal process, but I do think there is a place for open-ended questions about a person's wellbeing, offering them the opportunity to broach any difficult subjects they wish to discuss. You can avoid making it personal: if you have a holistic approach to wellbeing as an organization and it is a shared understanding that physical, mental, and spiritual wellbeing are inextricably bound together, then it is natural and legitimate to discuss these issues together, including our approach to food and its impact upon us individually and collectively.

You can do this when you plan the menus for a community event or a weekend away, and when you consider what food and drink is served at team meetings or after a church service. This way you avoid lecturing. You are showing, not telling. Instead of ending up with the example I described earlier of the overweight leadership team, the result is more likely to be a healthier, positive, collective mindset.

3. Lead by example

You can only set the culture if you lead by example. I've already referred to the importance of vital, visible leadership. I'm not just throwing down a challenge to religious leaders here, but to all leaders, including medical ones. The public still looks up to NHS workers and expects them to set an example. Sadly, there is a high prevalence of obesity among health professionals, particularly nurses and care workers.[16] If you've read Spiderman comics or seen the films, you will be familiar with the concept that with power comes responsibility. As a leader you put yourself forward into the spotlight. Believing that you can expect others to do what you say but not as you do is naive and hypocritical. If there is work that you need to do on yourself, and support that you need from others as part of this process, then step up, ask for help, and do it. If you're not prepared to lead by example, ask yourself how this affects the community that you profess to serve, and why you are leading at all. You have the opportunity to challenge any unhealthy, default norms and set new ones.

This has been the most difficult chapter of the book for me to write: partly because there's a lot of information out there, and conflicting interpretations to go with it; and partly because I wanted to get the level right, providing enough detail to be credible and helpful, without going too deeply into the depths of dietary obsession. I'm also aware that it is one of the issues with which people identify most commonly, when they are struggling with their wellbeing and wanting to make changes. I hope that I've given you enough food for thought (another intentionally poor pun) and ideas to help you make a plan and take the next steps, and that I've more or less managed to straddle the line between being both sensitive and challenging when it comes to this complicated issue.

Remember that you are loved by your creator, who doesn't judge you for what you put on your fork. We all have different life experiences and the pain that we can carry as a result. Your fate is not sealed. You can take control by just starting with very simple changes. Being kind to yourself is very important. You are worthy of love and one way of showing this to yourself is by eating well.

Notes

1. Yuval Noah Harari, *Sapiens: A Brief History of Humankind* (New York: Harper, 2015).

2. Mark Hyman, *Food: WTF should I eat? A No-Nonsense Guide to Achieving Optimal Weight and Lifelong Health* (London: Hodder & Stoughton, 2018).

3. Michael Greger, *How Not to Die: Discover the Foods Scientifically Proven to Prevent and Reverse Disease* (New York: Flatiron Books, 2015).

4. World Health Organization, *World Health Statistics 2016: Monitoring health for the SDGs*. Available at: https://www.who.int/gho/publications/world_health_statistics/2016/en.

5. Global, Regional, and National Incidence, Prevalence, and Years Lived with Disability for 328 Diseases and Injuries for 195 Countries, 1990–2016: A Systematic Analysis for the Global Burden of Disease Study 2016, *The Lancet*, 390 (2017), 1211–59.

6. 'Homicide in England and Wales: Year ending March 2018,' Office for National Statistics. Available at: https://www.ons.gov.uk/peoplepopulationandcommunity/crimeandjustice/articles/homicideinenglandandwales/yearendingmarch2018.

7. Michael Pollan, *In Defense of Food: An Eater's Manifesto* (New York: Penguin, 2008).

8. World Cancer Research Fund, *Diet, Nutrition, Physical Activity and Cancer: A Global Perspective*. The Third Expert Report, 2017. Available at: https://www.wcrf.org/dietandcancer. Accessed 19.10.2020

9. John Yudkin, *Pure, White and Deadly: The Problem of Sugar* (London: Davis-Poynter, 1972).

10. L.R Saslow, C. Summers, J.E. Aikens, and D.J. Unwin, 'Outcomes of a Digitally Delivered Low-Carbohydrate Type-2 Diabetes Self-Management Program: 1-Year Results of a Single-Arm Longitudinal Study', *JMIR Diabetes*, 3: 3 (2018), e12.

11. Malcolm Kendrick, *A Statin Nation: Damaging Millions in a Brave New Post-health World* (John Blake, 2019).

12. Numbers Needed to Treat (NNT), Statins for Heart-Disease Prevention Without Prior Heart Disease. Available at: https://www.thennt.com/nnt/statins-for-heart-disease-prevention-without-prior-heart-disease-2.

13. A.E. Buyken and J. Brand-Miller, 'Carbohydrates and inflammation', in Manohar Garg and Lisa Wood, *Nutrition and Physical Activity in Inflammatory Diseases* (University of Australia: 2012), pp. 46–60.

14. G.L. Palmisano, M. Innamorati, and J. Vanderlinden, 'Life Adverse Experiences in Relation with Obesity and Binge Eating Disorder: A Systematic Review'. *Journal of Behavioral Addictions*, 5: 1 (2016), 11–31.

15. M. Lenoir, F. Serre, L. Cantin, and S.H. Ahmed, 'Intense Sweetness Surpasses Cocaine Reward', *PLOS ONE*, 2: 8 (2007), art. no. e698.

16. R.G. Kyle, J. Wills J., C. Mahoney, et al., 'Obesity Prevalence among Healthcare Professionals in England: A Cross-Sectional Study Using the Health Survey for England', *British Medical Journal Open*, 7: e018498 (2017).

7. Movement

For in him we live and move and have our being.
(Acts 17: 28, KJV)

The miracle drug

Imagine the CEO of a global pharmaceutical company sitting in their office contemplating where the next billion-dollar drug is going to come from when one of their researchers comes rushing in. They are almost incoherent with excitement and babbling something about a miracle drug. Intrigued, the CEO persuades them to take off their lab coat and goggles, sit down and take a few deep breaths, and tell them more about this breakthrough. The researcher explains that they have discovered the most amazing drug. It can prevent, reverse, cure, or control most of what ails us. It is non-toxic, with almost nothing in the way of side effects, and can be taken by anyone, regardless of their state of health. It doesn't have any dangerous interactions with other treatments that they may be taking and can be delivered in a variety of ways to suit the user. There's no need for any costly or time-consuming trials on animals or humans, because that research has already been done and there is publicly available data stretching back thousands of years. Weirdly, despite all this evidence, the drug is not currently being used by most people, not on a regular basis anyway. So, there's an opportunity to really grow the market. Best of all, it doesn't cost anything to make, to package or to distribute to the end user.

By now, the CEO is pretty excited too. The literal billion-dollar question is, of course, what the company can charge for this miracle drug. What will their margin be? Presumably, if it costs nothing to make, it could be 100 per cent? This could change the world, secure their place in history, and make them rich beyond their wildest dreams! Unfortunately, as the legal and finance team will tell them after looking into it, there's bad news. Bad news for the company, but really good news for the entire world. There is very little money in this miracle drug. It's free to everyone at the point of access. There's no intellectual property here to patent. They can try branding it and using fancy packaging, but so can all their competitors. To make things worse, there are non-profit public-sector organizations out there who are already promoting and providing this product. How many people will be willing to pay for something that they can have for free? The shareholders are unlikely to approve. Disappointed, the CEO sends the researcher away, reflecting that there's a good reason why these people aren't normally allowed out of the lab and making a note to have this brought up at their next appraisal.

The miracle drug that our putative CEO was contemplating briefly goes by different names. Traditionally we have used terms such as 'exercise' or 'physical activity'. I like to describe it to my patients simply as 'movement'.

We are made to move

It doesn't matter whether you believe that we are designed by a creator, or the end product of millions of years of random mutations and natural selection. What is absolutely true, regardless of your creed or philosophy, is that we are made to move. It is who we are and what we do. Think about how you feel if you've been sitting still for too long. No matter how comfortable your chair, at some point you will feel restless and uncomfortable. You start by trying to shift your position and by stretching but sooner or later you will get up and move. That's what movement is: simply a change in position or place.

I used to believe that our natural resting state was literally resting and that movement was something that we had to make an effort to do as we forced ourselves away from this natural state. As a junior doctor I perceived exercise as something that was a deliberate and possibly not entirely pleasant act, a departure from the norm, even a necessary evil. What I've learnt from almost a quarter of a century of clinical practice is that I was looking at it the wrong way round. It's actually movement that is our default setting. It's easy enough to extoll the virtues of movement and I will of course do exactly that in this chapter, but what is even more compelling, when it comes to making the argument for it being our default setting, is looking at what happens when we deprive ourselves of it and suffer from what I describe as 'Movement Deficiency Disorder' (MDD).

Do you suffer from Movement Deficiency Disorder?

Rather than being an optional add-on to our lives that some may choose to avoid, movement is an integral, fundamental part of our wellbeing. The problems caused by deficiency of sleep, water, oxygen, vitamins, and sunlight are well understood. So it is with movement, and our understanding of its importance is increasing. When I first came up with the term 'movement deficiency disorder' I assumed that someone else had done so already. However, the internet didn't come up with anything when I searched for it, which surprised me. In the medical world, diseases are listed and defined in various manuals that are updated on a regular basis. On the basis that we are now dignifying losing our temper or spending too much time online as *medical* conditions, I'm definitely claiming this one. So now I'd like you to spend a few moments thinking about whether you might be a sufferer. To help, I've put together this list of symptoms and signs of MDD.

I'm going to start with a disclaimer: no one is perfect and nor will our choices always be. In fact, sometimes we deliberately choose *not* to choose what might be considered the right thing. That's fine, in moderation. You're not a bad person if you haven't done 10,000 steps today. That said, ask yourself whether and how often the following might apply to you or to those that you know:

- Avoidance of physical activity.

- Shortness of breath and raised heart rate on minimal exertion.

- Sleeping poorly.

- Aches and pains in your joints.

- Struggling to get out of your chair.

- Loss of confidence (physically or mentally).

- Turning down a social occasion that would involve physical activity.

- Feeling low or anxious.

- Feeling too tired to be physically active.

- Feeling older than your years.

Or have you developed any of the following long-term conditions: obesity, osteoarthritis, raised blood pressure, diabetes, heart disease, depression, or dementia?

Do any of these raise any red flags or alarm bells? They can be something of a vicious circle or a chicken-and-egg scenario of course. Sometimes it can be hard to tell whether these experiences and behaviours are caused by movement deficiency or if movement deficiency is caused by these experiences and behaviours. The end result is the same – a spiralling down into inertia. Fortunately, the reverse is also true. If you can start to move more, in however small and simple a way, you can start to rise up and eventually take off.

The toxic death cult of convenience

I used to see our society and the environment in which we live as a neutral or even benign one when it came to movement. I thought that on average in everyday life I would almost inevitably be physically active enough to stay fit and well. Growing up in the 1970s and 1980s, it was much less common to encounter people who were very seriously overweight and unfit, but it wasn't unknown. There was of course a child in every class who got picked on. That was partially because attitudes were less kind, but also because they were probably the only one in the class. If I'm honest, I will admit that like many of my classmates I labelled them, subconsciously or even out loud, as 'fat' and 'lazy'. It was the age of inconvenience. Everyone in my class walked to the local primary school and the shops. Most childhood socializing was based around physical activities and we spent long days chasing each other round the block on bikes, kicking a ball around, playing variations of hide and seek, climbing trees or stealing balls in commando-style raids from the back of the eighteenth hole of the local golf course. Mobile phones didn't exist, even for Porsche-driving yuppies (who were not yet called 'yuppies'). Games consoles in the home were not yet commonplace, most families did not have personal computers, and the World Wide Web was still just a twinkle in Tim Berners-Lee's eye.

There has been a shift towards lives that involve much less movement day to day. From our modern-day perspective, it may appear to be a slow drift, occurring over decades, in which we have gradually become less active. In terms of the length of time during which humans have been on the planet, it's actually very rapid as it has taken place over the last hundred years or so against a backdrop of hundreds of thousands of years or more. Prior to the industrial revolution, physical activity was not just a necessity for working life and survival, it also played a big part in social life. For hunter-gatherers, there would be a natural rhythm to life which included short periods of intense physical activity followed by rest. Movement was not just essential for survival either. There would also be periods of longer, less intense movement, as people would walk long distances to meet up with family and celebrate important occasions. It doesn't really matter how you view it. Fast or slow, the consequences are current and have been catastrophic. Although it is easy to be judgemental, to point at individuals who are inactive, and to label them as lazy, we need to consider the bigger picture.

Imagine the difference between the life of an average person today and what it would have been 100 years ago. Today the average person is likely to be woken up by their smartphone, commute to a sedentary job inside an office block in an urban environment, eat prepared food on the go, commute back home again, and spend the end of the day sedentary and very likely staring at a screen. One hundred years ago they would have woken up with the sun, spent a day performing manual labour, travelled without the use of a motor, eaten wholefood (probably grown at home), and spent the end of the day with family and friends, perhaps including physical activities for fun and relaxation, before going to bed when the sun went down. There's a big difference both between the lives of these two people and the quality of life they can expect as a result.

Although it's true that medical advances have increased our life span, they haven't increased our *health* span, which is the proportion of our lives that we can enjoy largely free from disease and associated limitations. This is a result of the dystopian, toxic environment which we have made for ourselves and in which we now live. You might think that these are strong words to use, conjuring up images from sci-fi books and films. However, to someone living 100 years ago, miracles of technology aside, the world we live in now might well look truly dystopian, straight from the pen of a writer.

Global research into the levels of physical inactivity of almost two million people, published in *The Lancet* in 2018, found that over a quarter of people were not physically active enough (defined by doing less than the amount recommended by the World Health Organization), and that this was more marked, and getting worse, in the richest countries.[1] Literally a first-world problem. It is likely to be an underestimate because it is based on surveys of what people remember or say. Even making the heroic assumption that the people who took part in the surveys were honest with themselves and others, we are still left with the question of how we measure that which we know nothing about. I suspect that the data from the billions of people who *didn't* take part in such surveys would make the figures worse rather than better.

In the UK, activity data for 2018 taken from a Sport England survey and analysed by Public Health England showed that 66 per cent of adults met the definition for being active.[2] You could argue that this isn't terrible, but it's an average for all adults and it gets a lot worse with age, dropping to 48 per cent at age 75, and to 26 per cent at age 85. It was also worse with deprivation, dropping from 72 per cent in the least deprived areas, to 57 per cent in the most deprived. One of the problems here is the widely held assumption among both the medical profession and the general public that physical activity will decline inevitably with age. The term 'sarcopenia' is defined as the age-related loss of skeletal muscle mass and function. The causes of this are many and include chronic diseases and inflammation, but what is worth noting is that the first cause listed in most definitions is 'disuse'. Disuse is not a disease nor an inevitability. It's the consequence of culture and belief, presenting both a daunting challenge and an exciting opportunity.

If you think the figures for adults are bad, they're a lot worse for children. In the same survey just 18 per cent of children met the Chief Medical Officer's guidelines for physical activity, with 33 per cent doing half or less of the recommended amount of one hour a day. Girls were less active than boys, and once again deprivation made everything worse. It is well documented that physical activity declines into adulthood. So, if we have an adult population raised in an age of inconvenience, who were more active in childhood and are now struggling to move enough, how much worse will the situation be for today's children as they age?

This seismic shift in how much we move isn't because some isolated individuals have made the decision to go against public health advice and common sense. It's because the whole environment has changed and what we view as default normal behaviour has changed as a result. The problem we now face as a society is that laziness is not primarily an individual intentional lifestyle choice, it is learnt on a large scale. It's almost as if we have taken what we instinctively know to be true, backed up by thousands of years of instinct, wisdom, and evidence, and then decided to run headlong (or perhaps *shuffle* would be more appropriate) in the opposite direction. In the developed world we can see this in the way we have built our houses, schools, public transport system, and working environment. Technology, such a blessing when used in the right way, can also be a curse if we unthinkingly allow mission creep so that it invades our lives more and more, gradually eradicating the need to move at all. Ultimately, we are rendered weak and immobile, all in the name of convenience.

There is a word that can be used to describe a group of people that show unthinking devotion and veneration towards an object or goal: a 'cult'. I believe that, without realizing it, we have become members of, or are at risk of being sucked into, a cult of convenience. And not just any old cult, but a toxic death cult. As bad as this is for our wellbeing as adults who have been inducted into the cult, it's potentially a lot worse for our kids, who have been born into it, brainwashed from birth. Now you may be thinking that I'm coming on a bit strong, but bear with me as I describe the consequences of being in this cult, before moving on to considering how we might plan our escape.

The inevitable consequences of Movement Deficiency Disorder (MDD)

Although I don't believe that MDD is inevitable, the consequences of it are. Put very simply, these are disease and death. The list of problems caused by, or made more likely by inactivity is a long one. For the sake of time, I'll shorten it down to just obesity, high blood pressure, stroke, diabetes, heart disease, cancer, depression and anxiety, dementia, poor sleep, falls, fractures, deteriorating physical function, and generally growing old before your time.

We don't stop moving because we grow old. We grow old because we stop moving. You might think that one way of overcoming sitting still all day is to blast away at the gym in the evening. You'd be wrong. Even people who achieve recommended daily levels of moderate to vigorous physical activity are harmed by prolonged sitting, and so far it has not been possible to produce evidence-based recommendations for how much physical activity is required to overcome this effect.[3] For me, the take-home message here is that the decisions we make about how much we sit or move have parallels with the decisions we make about what we eat. Rather than trying to work out how far you have to run to overcome sitting still, or how many apples you should eat to compensate for that chocolate bar, you're better off avoiding the problem to start with. You can't outrun a sedentary lifestyle.

Being sedentary won't just reduce the quality of your life, it will shorten it too. Inactivity has been described as the new smoking. It's the fourth leading cause of death around the world — twice as bad as obesity.[4] Moving isn't just a life-prolonging bonus activity. It's an essential nutrient, a vitamin whose deficiency leads to a shorter and less enjoyable life.

So far, so gloomy. I don't know about you, but I've depressed myself just writing these last few paragraphs. We're desperately in need of some good news. Thankfully, the good news about the good news is that there's plenty of it. Let's get back to this miracle drug . . .

Movin' in the free world

Back at the beginning of this chapter I started by describing this miracle drug before listing all the perils of not having enough of it in our lives. Following the logical rules of cause and effect, introducing more of it back into our lives, restoring movement to its natural and rightful place, will result in less disease, improved function, and a better life. I emphasize to my patients that this is a key feature of managing, recovering from, or reversing their health problems, such as obesity, hypertension, pre-diabetes and diabetes, heart disease, arthritis, cancer, depression, anxiety, and dementia. There is something special and protective about physical activity, which goes above and beyond the side effects we can measure, such as reduced weight, cholesterol, blood pressure, or blood sugar. Even allowing for these variables or 'confounding factors' (a term used in research to describe things other than your intended treatment, which might influence the outcomes of a study), there is an additional benefit to our wellbeing above and beyond this. Let's look at some numbers related to movement and its benefits, starting with doing very little and working our way up.

Did you know that simply standing for two hours a day reduces your risk of dying, from any cause, by 10 per cent?[5] Let's just think about that for a moment. Standing requires absolutely nothing other than the ability to stay upright, for short periods of time. This skill is possessed by the vast majority of people over the age of 1, on the face of this planet. I like to think of myself as something of an expert in this area, which I have achieved without any special training at all. I haven't seen any standing classes at the gym or in the park recently. I prescribe drugs to my patients to lower blood pressure and cholesterol. They will probably take them every day for the rest of their lives. They have side effects and require regular monitoring, including blood tests. For many people, these pills will reduce risk less effectively than standing for two hours every day. I don't know about you, but I know which option I'd prefer if given the choice.

Did you know that you don't have to 'exercise' to get health benefits? Let's define physical activity as muscle movement; exercise as purposeful physical activity to improve fitness; and fitness as the ability to perform and enjoy life's activities. Health benefits occur as a result of 'non-exercise' physical activity.[6] There is no threshold, no level of movement below which there is no benefit. Something is better than nothing.

Talking about risk and percentages is all well and good, but the more absolute benefits, such as living a longer and healthier life, are the real selling point to most of us. So, it may interest you to know that the average person doing moderate physical activity, such as a brisk walk, for 90–150 minutes a week – roughly in line with the Chief Medical Officer's current recommendations – can expect to live for an extra two-and-half years.[7] That's a big deal! Stop for a minute to think about all that has happened in the last two-and-half years in your life. Think about what you could do with that time, or all that you might miss out on if you didn't have it. Just in case you are inclined to sniff at an extra two-and-a-half years of life, finding it a marginal gain, let us consider the case for statins (cholesterol-lowering drugs). In a review published in *The British Medical Journal*, it was calculated that the typical gain in life expectancy, in a variety of studies running for somewhere between two and six years, was – wait for it! – just over three days. No, that's not a typo. Or as Dr Malcolm Kendrick, author of *The Great Cholesterol Con* and *A Statin Nation*, puts it: if you take a statin for thirty years you might live for about two years longer.[8] So, which do you prefer? A pill every day with potential side effects, drug interactions, and blood tests, or the superior treatment of brisk walking for 18 to 30 minutes a day, with weekends optional? While you weigh this one up, I'm off to look up the dictionary definition for 'no-brainer'.

There is also evidence that more intense physical activity (described as high-intensity interval training, or HIIT) might be even more beneficial, giving us equivalent benefits that it would take us perhaps twice as long to realize with moderate physical activity, hence the recommendations of around 150 minutes of moderate or 75 minutes of high intensity physical activity per week.[9] There are apps that you can download specifically to take you through HIIT workouts, which can easily be done in your home with minimal equipment. I recommend these to younger people who are already at least moderately active, as they can be a bit brutal, at least to the uninitiated, and carry with them a higher risk of injury. They can be a good option if you wake up in the morning to discover that the weather outside is bad and you've overslept!

Although research data gathered from randomized controlled trials, observational studies, and surveys is useful and give us a good basis for our decision-making and life choices, they can be a bit dry. Research conditions aren't always easy or desirable to replicate in everyday life. The people that take part in such research themselves may be self-selecting and perhaps not representative of the general population around them. They may lie when they fill in the survey about how physically active they are, making some of the results questionable. So how can we see the benefits of movement in the real world? One answer lies in the study of the 'Blue Zones'.

'Blue Zones' is the term used to describe regions around the world where people live an unusually long time. The original five blue zones were identified as Sardinia (Italy), Okinawa (Japan), Nicoya (Costa Rica), Icaria (Greece), and Loma Linda (California). The population in these areas includes an unusually high proportion of those living for more than 100 years. Perhaps more importantly, these centenarians enjoy not just a long lifespan but a long health span, suffering fewer of the diseases that will affect many of us. If you would like to know more, I recommend Dan Buettner's book on the subject, written after his research on the blue zones for *National Geographic*.[10] We will be coming back to the blue zones later, but the point I want to emphasize here is that one of the common ingredients for longevity, identified in each and every blue zone, was constant, moderate physical activity. These are communities that live lives of inconvenience, from which they benefit hugely. They are active all day long. By that I mean that movement is an intrinsic part of their day, at work or at play. They don't have gym subscriptions, treadmills, or military fitness camps. They are on the go, all the time. They don't stop because they get old. It's because they don't stop that they age well. This leads us nicely onto considering what place movement should have in our lives. We may not be fortunate enough to live in an original blue zone, but we can take the principles and apply them to our own lives, in our own communities.

If movement is a miracle drug, what's the right dose?

There are people out there who, if asked this question, will launch into a lengthy and complicated answer. Many of these same people do this because they are 'experts' in the subject, and (more to the point) their livelihoods depend on it being something that mere mortals couldn't possibly do for themselves. Moreover, those mortals will undoubtedly require their assistance with it, ideally, having taken out a subscription and purchased a book, some activewear, training paraphernalia, and food supplements – preferably all of them. I don't begrudge people the opportunity to make a living, but the very bad news for them and the very good news for the rest of us is that it's really simple. Here are my three principles of motion, inspired by Sir Isaac Newton, only much easier to remember and with no equations:

My first principle of motion is: *our natural state is to be in motion.* Whereas the body described by Sir Isaac in his first law remained in a state of rest unless acted on by an external force, your body's natural default position is one of movement. Although we do need some periods of rest and sleep, these should not make up most of our day. To be forced to spend so much time sitting or lying down is unnatural and ultimately harmful for our physical, mental, and spiritual wellbeing. The reason that so many of us do this is because, whether we realize it or not, we have been indoctrinated by the death cult. Many of today's children have been born into the factory farm of convenience, penned in by indolence because they don't know what life could really be like. This change of mindset is fundamental. We need to break free and range freely to live as we are meant to and enjoy a full life.

My second principle of motion is: *some is better than none.* Taking those first steps away from the couch, or making the decision to become increasingly active, is both vital and simple. Starting to become more physically active can seem a very daunting prospect for someone who breaks into a sweat at the mere thought of breaking into a sweat. Standing at the bottom of a mountain, craning your neck to see the summit and watching expert mountaineers toiling up the slopes armed with all their climbing gear can be pretty daunting, and you might be forgiven for not even starting. Fortunately, the evidence for the benefits of increasing movement favours the inactive, not the highly active. By this I mean that the greatest reduction in the risk of death and disease is seen in those who go from being inactive to mildly active. The biggest benefit is felt by those who literally take their first few steps off the couch and down the street or the end of the garden, not those who go from jogging 5km to running marathons. In a study published in the *British Medical Journal* the key findings were that increasing your level of activity, at whatever level of intensity, and spending less time sedentary, significantly reduces your likelihood of dying from any cause.[11] Not just heart disease or diabetes or cancer – *any* cause. Interestingly, there may be a maximum therapeutic dose of movement. There is very little benefit of doing much more than two hours a week of moderate physical activity. After this the risks of injury increase. David Spiegelhalter is a statistician and the Winton Professor of the Public Understanding of Risk, at the University of Cambridge. In his excellent book, *The Norm Chronicles*, he describes micromorts and microlives; units he has made up to measure the harms or benefits of the things that we do.[12] According to his calculations, the first 20 minutes of moderate intensity physical activity pay dividends and extend our life. After 20 minutes we break even. There is no benefit to life expectancy much beyond this, which fits roughly with the idea of the 30 minutes a day recommendation from the Chief Medical Officer.

So, if you like running ultra-marathons or climbing mountains, be honest with yourself about why you do it. It might be good for the soul, but you probably won't live any longer, particularly if you fall over and break something, or fall off the mountain you are climbing. Like any medicine, physical activity should be taken in the right dose. Too much of anything, even water or oxygen, is bad for you.

My third principle of motion is: *everyone needs a different dose*. Any doctor will tell you that giving someone too much medicine and increasing the dose too quickly is likely to result in unpleasant side effects and the patient deciding to stop taking it. The 'start low, go slow' approach that the medical profession adopts to try and avoid this with medication is exactly how we should approach increasing the amount of movement in our lives. Having accepted the truth and adopted the mindset resulting from the first principle, and then started to restore movement to its rightful place in our lives with the second principle, it is vital we follow the third to make it a sustainable way of life.

Most of us may be aware of the Chief Medical Officer's guidelines recommending that we do 150 minutes of moderate intensity, or 75 minutes of high-intensity physical activity per week.

Moderate physical activity gets your heart rate up. It makes you breathe a little harder and faster, and feel warm. Examples include brisk walking, gardening, cycling, dancing, or heavy housework. Higher-intensity activities include running, circuit training, aerobics, spinning, and playing sports. However, the latest version of the guidelines is pragmatic and recognizes that we will all need to approach this as individuals. You might start with shorter sessions lasting a few minutes rather than half an hour. You may not have the same opportunities every day because of your diary. You may prefer to look at measures that are more about integrating movement naturally into your life in a rational, relevant, and routine way rather than considering doing 'exercise'. Some people will be encouraged by joining a gym or a club, or doing something with a friend or family member. Using fancy clothing, smartphone apps, or other equipment can be motivating and enjoyable for some. Just putting on a pair of trainers and taking the dog out is what does it for others. No one will take medicine that tastes bad, not in the long term anyway. To be sustainable, it must be meaningful and rewarding.

What can we learn about movement from the Bible?

Having conducted exhaustive research I was disappointed to find that there is nothing in scripture referring to the benefits of high-intensity interval training. Nor did Jesus say, 'Blessed are those who smash their Parkrun personal best, for they shall win Strava.' We can, however, learn from how movement featured in everyday life, and from biblical teaching that uses movement as an illustration.

Spiritual health is often equated to good physical health

One goes hand in hand with the other.

> They who wait for the Lord shall renew their strength;
> they shall mount up with wings like eagles; they shall
> run and not be weary; they shall walk and not faint.
> (Isaiah 40: 31, ESV)

> I have fought the good fight, I have finished the race.
> I have kept the faith. (2 Timothy 4: 7, NIV)

Worship was also a very physical experience

At no point does the psalmist write, 'Oh Lord, you are so great that I feel moved to express this by ... doing absolutely nothing. For hours at a time'. Worship might involve bowing, kneeling, and lying prostrate, but it also includes singing, dancing, clapping hands, and raising arms. It is an instinctive response to how we feel and need to express ourselves.

The value of discipline is also recognized

You can't have control over your life if you don't have control over your body. The example we set to others, regardless of our status or belief system, is telling and affects our credibility.

> But I discipline my body and keep it under control,
> lest after preaching to others I myself should be
> disqualified. (1 Corinthians 9: 27, ESV)

We should persist

If we find physical activity tough at the time we are doing it, we should look at it from a longer-term perspective and think about what our future selves would thank us for.

> **For the moment all discipline seems painful rather than pleasant but later it yields the peaceful fruit of righteousness to those who have been trained by it. Therefore lift your drooping hands and strengthen your weak knees. (Hebrews 12: 11f, ESV)**

I could go on about how Jesus and his disciples walked everywhere, stood a lot, preached all day, and had physical jobs like fishing and carpentry, but of course so did most people in those times. We can only speculate whether Jesus would have used an electric scooter or been Ubered between delivering parables had such options been available. However, it is worth noticing that even in times of constant moderate physical activity, the value of going further and pushing harder was recognized. As the Apostle Paul says:

> **Let us run with endurance the race that is set before us, looking to Jesus, the founder and perfecter of our faith. (Hebrews 12: 1–3, ESV)**

What is your movement culture?

Let's now consider both the challenges and how we can overcome them in our communities, whether as a church or other faith-based organization. If you are a leader, are you leading by example? Is it obvious to those that you serve that being physically active is an important part of your whole life and you aren't artificially dividing the physical from the spiritual? When you preach to others about the importance of discipline and self-control, are you credible? Do other people believe you? Do you believe yourself?

Think about the role of movement in meetings and community events. Are they sedentary and prolonged affairs? Do people have the opportunity to be physically active in them, not just because it's 'healthy', but because you've made it an integral part of the discussion and teaching? It's absolutely right to make sure that those with disabilities for whom movement is more difficult can access group activities and get the most out of them. We should apply the same principle to everyone else, including those that would benefit from moving more.

If you work with young people you have a particularly important role to play. You are a role model and can inspire them and teach them lessons that will stick with them for the rest of their lives. Do you make sure that movement is built into the weekly timetable and any special events that you are organizing? I have fond memories of youth clubs, whether in a faith or secular setting. We played darts, pool, table football, table tennis, dodgeball, and rag hockey indoors. Outdoors we would play wide games, rounders, and football, and go for walks and camping weekends. When you are leading a teaching session, or having a group discussion, do you talk about what it means to be physically as well as spiritually active? I believe that we shouldn't see these as separate issues, but rather as two sides of the same coin.

My prescription for moving more

For individuals

1. Make movement a natural part of your day

Before you even start pondering a gym membership and whether you look good in Lycra, think about the things you can do that will make it as painless and easy to do as possible. This way you can move away from thinking of movement as 'exercise', which is a barrier for some people. Use the stairs more at home and at work. Consider the lift a device reserved exclusively for those who are unable to walk, or who are carrying heavy loads.

Walk or cycle to work or get off the train/Tube/bus a stop or two early and walk the rest of the way. If you have to drive to work, think about getting up 20 minutes earlier to leave time for a brisk walk to get the day off to a good start. Get up from your desk or sofa every 30–60 minutes to walk around and stretch for a minute or two.

Drink plenty of water, which will both hydrate you and mean you have to walk to the bathroom more often too. Getting a dog guarantees you will end up getting more exercise as they will appoint themselves your trainer and will insist on you getting out of the house at least once a day. Another benefit is that having a dog will, in my opinion, make you a nicer person and result in you mixing with other nice people as well!

2. Take every opportunity to exercise

Note that I am using the bogey-word here because I'm referring to purposeful physical activity to improve fitness. You can exercise anywhere. You don't need equipment. Even in the office you can do micro-workouts where you might do 30–60 seconds of squats, lunges, sit-ups, press-ups (against your desk if you don't fancy the floor), or use some light weights you could keep on your desk or coffee table. These are all examples of strength-training exercises, which are recommended as part of your regular physical activity in addition to aerobic exercise, such as walking, running, swimming, and cycling. To get you started, I recommend you watch Dr Rangan Chatterjee's *5-Minute Kitchen Workout* on YouTube.

3. Start from where you are and do a little more

Anyone spending too much time staring at copies of *Men's Health*, adorned with images of specimens with six packs you could bounce a brick off, is likely to develop an inferiority complex and wonder where to even start. Remember my second law of motion, which states that something is better than nothing. As you feel the physical and mental benefits of being more active, you will inevitably find yourself wanting to do more and do better in this and other areas of your life. Start with a five-minute walk each day if you need to. Build up gradually to avoid injury or disappointment. If something you try doesn't work, don't give up. Try something different or take it more gently.

4. Use incentive bundling

This is the principle of attaching something you find rewarding to the habit you wish to form. Examples include watching your favourite Netflix box set, or listening to your favourite playlist, when on the treadmill or after an activity. If you are saving money by spending less on petrol, train tickets, and parking as you become more active, why not identify something special to spend it on, just for you? Habits are much more likely to form if we find them rewarding.

5. Socialize it

For the majority of people, connection with others through physical activity is likely to encourage them to keep it up. This could be something you do with family, friends, or others who share your interests. This works partly because it makes it more enjoyable, and partly because you have other people to whom you are making yourself accountable, such as a running or yoga club, or a fitness instructor, for example. Personally, I can't imagine anything I would like less than dragging a huge tyre around a park like an idiot while being shouted at by another idiot wearing army fatigues, but each to their own. Smart devices and apps can be particularly useful here for those of us who like to compete against ourselves or others.

6. Make a plan if you want to make it happen

Be specific. If you want to move more, think about what your goal is (e.g. to be able to play football with your kids or grandkids, feel more energetic each day, take part in your first Parkrun). Break it down into simple steps as to how you will achieve it, starting with putting protected time in your diary. Consider who you will tell about this, and who might, with your consent, hold you accountable and encourage you. Might it be your partner, a family member, a work colleague, or a leader at your church, synagogue, or mosque? Think about possible barriers to you achieving your goal, such as expense, time restrictions, your work environment, or the weather, and plan how you would overcome them in advance. This may well shape your choice about how you move more and what sort of activities you decide to do. After all, the best medicine is the one that you actually take.

For organizations and leaders

1. Lead by personal example

Be open with others about the place that movement has in your life and the things that work (or don't work) for you. Be clear if this is an area you struggle with. You don't need to be ripped to be taken seriously. You don't need to be perfect to serve and inspire others, but you do need to be honest. A leader admitting their flaws and seeking help and advice can inspire others to do the same, and feel that it is something attainable. I've seen entire leadership teams change both for better and for worse when it comes to physical fitness, depending on the examples being set.

2. Set the movement culture

It's not just the message that's given in church on a Sunday morning that counts, it's how we work, rest, and play the rest of the week that determines whether it means anything. If you are a leader, do you actively encourage your leadership team and congregation to prioritize movement in their personal and professional lives? If you are having a meeting, consider whether it could a standing or walking meeting. In fact, why not make this the default setting and instead, consider a meeting in which everyone spends the whole time sitting down an exceptional and unusual one? You'll spend a lot less time staring at PowerPoint and spreadsheets, for which everyone is likely to be grateful. When you are conducting an appraisal or setting targets, why not agree something specific with your appraisee about movement and fitness? This is very powerful because it shows that you consider this a priority and gives them permission to consider this an important part of their professional life.

3. Use the environment

Think about what opportunities are presented to you by your physical place of worship. If you have a lift in your building, why not put up a sign stating that it is for the exclusive use of those who are unable to use the stairs? There are organizations that specialize in workplace wellbeing, who will carry out assessments and make recommendations. One such example is Step Jockey. Using their website, you can print out customized signs to encourage stair use, which state how many calories you will burn by taking the stairs and emphasize the health benefits of doing so. You can even download an app which allows you to gamify this, introducing a competitive aspect for individuals or teams.

If your congregation is used to gathering for tea and coffee after a service, maybe just leave out enough tables and chairs for the small number that actually need them. Encourage everyone else to stand, reminding them that, as we now know, it will reduce their risk of dying. Although it's comforting to know that one day, they will meet their maker in heaven, they may not necessarily be in a rush to get there.

4. Plan ahead

If you have an event such as a community day or a weekend away, think about how you structure it to leave time for movement at regular intervals throughout the day. Put them in the diary and label them specifically. If you have a site with multiple venues (such as campsite or large building), you could space out the locations and give people more time to walk between them. If you are having a multifaith event, why not spread it across multiple places of worship, encouraging people to walk between them? Inclusive physical group activities at the start of the day and throughout are fun, encourage people to connect with others, and also promote better learning and recall of the topics discussed.

I hope that you have found my movement tips helpful, whether just for yourself or for your community. Some may resonate with you, others may not. Real life is complicated and translating from theory into practice can be challenging, but also tremendously rewarding and satisfying. I hope that adopting just one or two of these will help you make your escape from the toxic death cult into a life of freedom which you can live to the full.

If as people of faith we are to go out into the world, wearing spiritual armour, running the race set before us with renewed strength, soaring like eagles and fighting the good fight, we need to be fit enough to do it, physically, mentally, and spiritually. The steps we take towards achieving this are both literal and metaphorical. If faith can move mountains, surely we can move ourselves!

Notes

1. R. Guthold, G. Stevens, L. Riley, and F. Bull, 'Worldwide Trends in Insufficient Physical Activity from 2001 to 2016: A Pooled Analysis of 358 Population-based Surveys with 1.9 Million Participants', *The Lancet*, 6: 10 (2018), E 1077–1086.

2. Public Health England, Statistics on Obesity, Physical Activity and Diet, England 2019. Available at: https://digital.nhs.uk/data-and-information/publications/statistical/statistics-on-obesity-physical-activity-and-diet/statistics-on-obesity-physical-activity-and-diet-england-2019/part-5-adult-physical-activity.

3. R. Patterson, E. McNamara, M. Tainio, *et al.* 'Sedentary Behaviour and Risk of All-Cause, Cardiovascular and Cancer Mortality, and Incident Type 2 Diabetes: A Systematic Review and Dose Response Meta-analysis', *European Journal of Epidemiology*, 33: 9 (2018), 811–29.

4. World Health Organization, 'Global Health Risks. Mortality and Burden of Disease Due to Selected Major Risks', 2009. Available at: https://www.who.int/healthinfo/global_burden_disease/GlobalHealthRisks_report_full.pdf?ua.

5. T.M. Eijsvogels, S. Molossi, D.C. Lee, M.S. Emery, and P.D. Thompson, 'Exercise at the Extremes: The Amount of Exercise to Reduce Cardiovascular Events', *Journal of the American College of Cardiology*, 67: 3 (2016). 316–329.

6. C. E. Matthews, A. L. Jurj, X.-O. Shu, H.-L. Li, G. Yang, Q. Li, Y.-T. Gao, and W. Zheng, 'Influence of Exercise, Walking, Cycling, and Overall Nonexercise Physical Activity on Mortality in Chinese Women', *American Journal of Epidemiology*, 165: 12 (2007), 1343–1350.

7. S.C. Moore, A.V. Patel, C.E. Matthews, et al. 'Leisure Time Physical Activity of Moderate to Vigorous Intensity and Mortality: A Large Pooled Cohort Analysis', *PLOS Medicine*, 9: 11 (2012), e1001335.

8. M. Kendrick, ' How Much Longer Will You Live If You Take a Statin?' Available at: https://drmalcolmkendrick.org/2015/10/27/how-much-longer-will-you-live-if-you-take-a-statin.

9. M.J. Gibala, J.P. Little, M.J. Macdonald, and J.A. Hawley, 'Physiological Adaptations to Low-Volume, High-Intensity Interval Training in Health and Disease', *Journal of Physiology*, 590: 5 (2012), 1077–1084.

10. Dan Buettner, *The Blue Zones: Lessons for Living Longer from the People Who've Lived the Longest* (Washington, DC: National Geographic, 2008), p. vii.

11. U. Ekelund, J. Tarp, J. Steen-Johannessen, et al. 'Dose-Response Associations between Accelerometry Measured Physical Activity and Sedentary time and All-Cause Mortality: Systematic Review and Harmonised Meta-analysis', *British Medical Journal*, 366 (2019), l4570.

12. Michael Blastland and David Spiegelhalter, *The Norm Chronicles: Stories and Numbers about Danger* (Profile Books, 2013).

8. A Renewed Mind

Do not be conformed to this world, but be transformed by the renewal of your mind. (Romans 12: 2, ESV)

Stress: where would we be without it?

I don't want a stress-free life. We all need a bit of stress in our lives. In the history of evolution, it has been vital for our survival. We tend to think about and discuss the term in a negative way, but we needn't. We wouldn't consider a colour or a temperature inherently bad, and neither is stress. It depends what purpose it serves. It's not so much the stress itself as our response to it. Thousands of years ago, we needed this mechanism to escape large hungry predators. Nowadays we might need it to help us compete in a sporting event, run for the bus, or make that important last-minute work deadline. Stress is like porridge in the story of *Goldilocks and the Three Bears*: we need just the right amount, neither too much nor too little, not too hot nor too cold. The problem for many of us is that we struggle to achieve this balance.

According to the Global Burden of Disease survey, conducted by the World Health Organization, anxiety and depression combined are the leading cause of years lost to disability, adding up to almost 10 per cent globally between them.[1] Stress, and the response to it over a prolonged period of time, plays a significant role in these mental health problems developing. If you think that sounds bad, you need to also consider that these two conditions are listed separately from the other top twenty causes of disability, including ischaemic heart disease, stroke, back and neck pain, and certain cancers – all of which may be contributed to by stress.

Let's talk about stress

So, if we need just the right amount of stress in our lives, but august bodies like the World Health Organization are warning us that it's also the greatest epidemic of the twenty-first century, how have we ended up here? We aren't born stressed to the eyeballs. How does it happen? Well, there are lots of reasons. We have considered the toxic, environmental default settings when it comes to sleep, food, and movement. It will, I hope, come as no surprise to you by now that there is a similar issue here. There are plenty of clues if you look for them. Let's break them down.

Back to basics

Let's start by reminding ourselves of a fundamental and unavoidable truth: body, mind, and spirit are all connected; physical, mental, and emotional wellbeing are inextricably linked. I have already highlighted the counterintuitive decisions that many of us make when it comes to our attitude to sleep, food, and movement. If we are not sleeping, eating, or moving it affects not just our physical but our mental wellbeing. It should therefore come as no surprise that whatever other factors come into play, we are at a disadvantage right out of the gate when it comes to mindset and mental wellbeing.

Life in the fast lane

Living in the developed world is a huge blessing. Most of us don't have to worry as much about things like infant mortality, communicable disease, access to food and water, a roof over our heads, and the right to live in peace, free from persecution and violence. In the race of life, we have started well ahead of the rest of the world. However, there is one respect in which we now find ourselves hugely disadvantaged, whether we realize it or not, and that is the pace of life and its consequences.

Most people reading this book will be living in an always-on, 24/7 culture. Life in the modern world is rapid and relentless. We have a 24-hour news cycle, delivered to our screens and pockets in a firehose of information. The speed with which this is delivered to us, whether at work or at home, appears to demand a similarly speedy response. Flexible working made possible by technology means that the once clear boundaries between work and home are now much more blurred. Working days are long and intense. It's not just our bosses who demand replies via email, it's our friends and family via our phones, SMS, WhatsApp, Facebook, Twitter, Instagram, Snapchat, Skype, WebEx, Zoom, and other platforms. But it gets worse.

It's not even just people that we know, people whom we have actual real-life relationships with, it's those with whom we have *virtual* relationships. Some of those are people, some are corporations, and some are just bots.

Digital technology has changed our world beyond recognition. Many of these changes are for the better. The ease and speed with which we can share information has made the impossible possible. When the Canadian astronaut Chris Hadfield was the commander of the International Space Station in 2013, I remember watching his video livestream from space as he played his version of 'Space Oddity' on his guitar. I did this when out shopping, using a device that fitted into my pocket, on which I could also check my email, send and receive messages, pay for my purchases, listen to music, and make phone calls using voice-activated commands – a device which makes the once-futuristic communicators in *Star Trek* look, frankly, a bit rubbish.

Such technology, in the developed world at least, is now taken for granted and viewed as ordinary, particularly by my children who are digital natives, born into *The Matrix*. They have never known any other world, whereas I, being in my forties, am a digital immigrant, who remembers the analogue world with one tethered landline in the hallway, VHS recorders, the Sony Walkman, the *Yellow Pages* phone directory, writing letters, and using a fax machine. I remember my first experience of digital home entertainment (*Pong*, played on my friend's Atari), my first home computer (the Spectrum 48k with rubber keys), my first CD (Dire Straits' *Brothers in Arms*), my first email address at university, and the very first time I surfed the World Wide Web from home, using a 56k modem that burbled as it tried to connect and was so slow that I could make myself a cup of tea as it did so.

I remember signing up for my first social-media account and what felt like liberation (he says, laughing hollowly) when I got my first iPhone, which meant I could now access the world from my pocket. I didn't consider that it also meant that the world could now access me.

The speed with which we have got from there to here is dizzying. I am grateful for this, but I am even more grateful for the perspective it gives me and the recognition that not all of this is good. Just as, when asked why they climb a mountain, climbers respond 'Because it's there', so we have used technology to do all sorts of things simply because we *can*, not necessarily because we *should*. The consequences were either not considered or perhaps simply couldn't be imagined. We have opened up Pandora's Can of Worms and can't get the lid back on. The irony of using such untethered technology is that we are now more tethered than ever, tracked and contactable wherever we go by, whether by our friends or by those whose intentions are more sinister.

Just in case it isn't already painfully obvious to you, tech giants like Google, Apple, and Facebook, who invented the devices and platforms that are ubiquitous today, are not benevolent entities, gently curious about where all of this might take us and without an agenda. They use every tool at their disposal, exploiting your FOMO (fear of missing out) and encouraging your addiction to the dopamine hit you get from someone 'liking' your post on social media, to suck you in and monetize you. If the service is free, then *you* are the product.

Like stress, technology is not inherently good or evil. It's a tool and it's what we do with it that matters. In the right hands, for things like awareness-raising, campaigns for social justice, and enabling us to communicate with our friends and family when they are dear but not near, it can be a great thing. However, there are significant risks of harm when it comes to mental wellbeing.

There is ongoing debate and the headlines change on a regular basis, but for me, there is enough evidence out there to be concerned. Although there isn't much in the way of randomized, controlled double-blind trials when it comes to the effects of social media, there are numerous surveys and reviews of the available data that have found a clear association among greater social-media use, online harassment, poor sleep, low self-esteem, poor body image, and worsening symptoms of depression. At the very least this indicates the need for caution and a much more considered approach to industry guidelines and regulations – and by this I mean actually having some – than we have adopted so far. We're playing a high-stakes game of catch-up.

The consequence of being always *on*, of trying to drink from the information firehose, is that we stop living intentionally and instead, by allowing constant intrusion into our thoughts and lives, we accept distraction as our default state. We don't give ourselves a moment's peace. We prevent ourselves from getting into 'the zone', the state of flow that is essential for us to be focused and productive in both our personal and professional lives. We are busily banning solitude from every moment of the day, scared of boredom, and utterly terrified at the prospect of being alone with our thoughts.

As finite beings, the more we fill our lives up with all of this stuff, the less time we have to rest and think. The less time we have to think, the more we become enslaved by habit and mindless behaviours, living life on autopilot with the volume gradually turning up to eleven.

The thieves of joy

Allow me to introduce you to the evil twins, Comparison and Expectation. They operate closely as a highly effective tag-team. Their mission is to steal your joy. They are very, very good at it.

When living your life in the fast lane, once your needs have been met (which, physically at least, applies to most of us), the next step is wants and desires. We compare ourselves to other people constantly, whether we realize it or not. There's a reason why not coveting (wanting what someone else has) made it into the Ten Commandments. It robs us of our joy and consumes us. It used to be the size of your neighbour's house, the state of their garden, how new their car was, and what sort of holidays they took. Now it includes their carefully curated Instagram feed and humble-bragging on Facebook.

We start by comparing ourselves with others. The possible becomes the available and desirable. Eventually we may feel that some things are a basic right, without which we will not be truly happy. This creates certain levels of aspiration and expectation. Please don't misunderstand me: there's nothing wrong with a bit of aspiration. There's something to be said for wanting a better world for ourselves and those around us, but the sunlit uplands of life – the place where you will exist in a steady state of peace, satisfaction, and fulfilment with no more sorrow or pain – are a myth and a mirage. In the book *Engineering Happiness*, the economist Rakesh Sarin describes a formula:[2]

Happiness = Reality - Expectation

The higher your expectations, the better reality is going to have to be for you to feel happy, and vice versa. Or to put it a different way, you can only enjoy true happiness if you are not consumed by the search for it. My own personal example of this is the television programme *Grand Designs*. I absolutely love it. In each episode the presenter Kevin McCloud follows the story of someone building their dream home. Whether it's the loving restoration of a ruined castle, the conversion of an old sewage works, or the creation an eco-house built into the landscape, these are all the passion projects of people building for a better life. There's often drama when things go wrong and the people concerned run out of money, or it takes much longer than planned, but the end results usually range from interesting to spectacular. My wife knows how much I love this programme and watching an episode on the couch with her is my reward if I have been particularly well behaved. We often talk about how we'd love to do something like this one day, when the kids have left home, and we are looking to downsize. Then it struck me the other day, when walking around our house and garden, that we already have our own 'grand design' – the place that we have lived for the last twenty years, home to our family of six. It has changed and grown with us, and is full of milestones and memories, some painful but mostly good. It's where we take refuge and comfort, entertain friends and family, and feel safe. Yes, there are bits that require improvement after twenty years, and other bits that we might change if time and finances permit. We have spent the most important time of our lives as a family here. We have been blessed and I remind myself of this every time I watch a happy (dare I say even just a little smug?) couple talking about realizing their lifelong vision of the perfect dwelling and how great their life is as a result.

It's important to remember, when you risk getting lost in comparison and expectation, when you are pinning all your hopes on the next experience, the next house, the next holiday, or life partner, that happiness is a journey, not a destination. We need to stop to smell the roses every now and again. We should remember to be grateful for what we have, however small or insignificant, instead of worrying about whatever we or those around us think we should have, but don't have yet.

Disconnection

Another source of stress and reason for deep-set unhappiness in modern society is the fragmentation of families and community, and the ascension of the cult of the individual. This is such an important issue, possibly the most important when it comes to what determines our wellbeing, that I have devoted Chapter 9 to it. For now, I will summarize by saying that as we have lost our connections with family, community, and faith, we have ended up with a world that is much more self-centred and much less happy. If I embrace the idea that there's no such thing as society, that I am the most important thing, then I end up playing a zero-sum game in which if I win, others have to lose. This does not make for a happy life. Not for most of us anyway. Life becomes an exhausting, soul-sapping battle as we look after Number One, seeking both to acquire what we don't yet have and, at the same time, clinging grimly on to what we do. Then, when things do go wrong in the race of life, the very connections that we need to survive and build resilience are the ones that we have weakened or severed in our attempt to get ahead and win it.

Inequality

We are all equal in the eyes of our creator. I would like to think that almost everyone on the face of this planet agrees with the principle of equality. Unfortunately, when it comes to the workings of everyday life, some of us are, in the words of George Orwell, 'more equal than others'. If you live in a developed nation like the UK or the USA then whatever challenges you may face in life you are already in the top few per cent of the global population when it comes to affluence. Of course, even within a relatively privileged society there are still inequalities, due to what are described in the medical and mental-health worlds as 'adverse life experiences'. Although neither experiences nor genetics set our destiny in stone, they can certainly shape a person's life course, and make it more or less likely that they will enjoy a good quality of life. Examples of such factors include poverty, homelessness, abuse, neglect, violence, long-term illness, and growing up in a household where adults have issues with their mental health, drugs, or alcohol. I referred earlier to the race of life. It's not so much a case of whether the playing field is level, but where the starting line is. Some of us will start ten paces ahead before we are even born, with others ten paces behind.

You've probably heard about banks conducting 'stress tests' to see how robust their financial systems are, like a sort of fire drill to see whether everyone makes it out into the car park on time, but on a huge corporate scale. Well, every now and then society unintentionally conducts a stress test. I'm writing this in the late summer of 2020, in the midst of the largest global stress test conducted in peacetime over the past 100 years, otherwise known as the Covid-19 pandemic. The world has been brought to its knees by a tiny virus.

One of the many consequences of the pandemic is that the gap between rich and poor has been cruelly exposed. Some have thrived in lockdown, working from comfortable home offices, or on furlough, surrounded by their family in nice houses with gardens, as they learn Mandarin and take up oil painting. Lockdown has been much grimmer for others coping with unemployment, financial difficulties, cramped accommodation with little or no access to green spaces, and social isolation. Whether it's physical, spiritual, or mental health, financial reserves or the quality of your relationships, the narrower your margin of safety – your buffer against the slings and arrows of misfortune – then the more inherently stressful life is. For many reasons, including some of those I have just described, more and more of us are living on this margin. It's not a comfortable place to be.

So now we've looked at stress on the macro scale in terms of its causes and effect on society, let's flip things around and go deeper, as we explore how it arises within, and affects, our cells and our bodies.

The stress pathway

It all starts with the input and processing of information. It could be something we see or hear, or a memory of what has happened previously. If we decide that a situation is stressful our brain activates the stress, or 'fight-or-flight' reaction, getting our body ready to do either. The amygdala, one of the oldest parts of our brains, sends a signal to another area, the hypothalamus, at the base of the brain. The hypothalamus acts as a sort of control centre. The resulting cascade of hormones results in the production of first adrenaline and then cortisol. The initial part of this pathway is instinctive, so fast that it occurs before we have even had a chance to fully make sense of what's happening. The hypothalamus communicates with our autonomic nervous system, a sort of autopilot for our body, which is in control of involuntary bodily functions.

If we were to compare our body to a car, the autonomic nervous system has both an accelerator pedal (the sympathetic nervous system) and a brake pedal (the parasympathetic nervous system). When our sympathetic nervous system is triggered it results in the heart beating faster and blood pressure rising to push more blood to our heart, muscles, and other vital organs. Our breathing rate increases and our airways open up so that we can take in more oxygen. Our senses become heightened. As the threat passes, our levels of cortisol fall. The parasympathetic nervous system applies the brakes and dampens everything down.

An acute stress reaction is appropriate and potentially life-saving. It's what makes us jump out of the way of the oncoming car before we even realize what is happening. A chronic one, however, is bad for our long-term wellbeing. Think about what that feels like: being on high alert most of the time, constantly prepared for flight or fight, lurching from moment to moment, surviving on instinct, unable to plan or rest. Symptoms of this may present bodily (headaches, muscle tension, chest pain, palpitations, fatigue, digestive upset, low sex drive, and disturbed sleep), mentally (anxiety, low mood, lack of motivation, irritability, and anger) or behaviourally (disordered eating, outbursts, use of alcohol and other drugs, social withdrawal, and becoming physically inactive).

One of the reasons that a chronic stress reaction is bad for us is that raised cortisol, produced in the fight-or-flight stage, suppresses levels of a protein called Brain-Derived Neurotrophic Factor (BDNF). BDNF was discovered in the 1980s and we now know it to be important in neurogenesis (the production of new nerve cells, including those in our brain) and neuroplasticity (the brain's ability to change itself and make new connections). It may also protect us against diseases of different body systems, whether in the brain (depression, Alzheimer's, Parkinson's), cardiovascular system (heart disease and diabetes), or gut (irritable bowel syndrome), although this is not yet fully understood and is the subject of ongoing research.

If these manifestations of the stress reaction were just short-term, unpleasant symptoms then it might not be such a big deal, just part of life's rich tapestry. Unfortunately, when this becomes chronic, there are long-term consequences, which we are learning more and more about.

Too much stress could kill you

Stress is now listed alongside inactivity, smoking, and obesity as a risk factor for a shorter, less happy life. There's plenty of available evidence. In an American study looking at daily stress and risk of death over a 20-year period, a correlation was found between stress levels and reduced life expectancy, regardless of social background, particularly in individuals with at least one chronic disease.[3] Another study published in the *British Journal of Psychiatry*, in 2018, found that the risk of dying from natural causes was increased by between 20 and 50 per cent in those suffering from anxiety, particularly if they also had depression.[4]

If you find percentages hard to get your head around, a study of Finnish men, published in the *British Medical Journal*, found that heavy levels of stress shortened their subjects' lives by almost three years.[5] That's a significant amount of opportunity lost. Think about how precious that time could be to you. The question now is not so much whether stress shortens your life, but *how* it does it. What is the pathway from stress to disease and death? The evidence points to our old friend and increasingly the usual suspect – inflammation.

Another inflammatory statement

Like stress, we need inflammation in our lives. It's an important part of our body's defence, helping us to fight infection and trauma, and is a fundamental part of the healing process. Like stress, you can have too much of it. Chronic stress can lead to chronic inflammation. Too much stress in your life means too much inflammation in your body.

There is growing evidence to support the theory that excessive levels of inflammation may be the common underlying cause of, or the contributing factor to, many different diseases, including heart disease, metabolic disease, neurological disease, mental health problems, and cancer. Raised levels of markers of inflammation can be found in our bodies with many of these conditions, including depression. Although it's possible that these markers could just be the end result of the inflammatory process and disease in question, it also appears that these inflammatory compounds can influence health and behaviour directly.

Inflammation in the brain may cause neurological diseases such as Parkinson's, dementia, and depression. In blood vessels it may cause cardiovascular disease, such as high blood pressure, heart attacks, and strokes. Inflammation may either stimulate or suppress the immune system, causing problems of over- or underactivity as a result. In the liver it may lead to liver disease, insulin resistance, and diabetes. Links have been made to specific cancers (including pancreas, breast, lung, liver, and blood), with regard to how tumours grow and spread. I'm deliberately restricting myself to an overview here, avoiding too much detail. However, if you would like to dig deeper, I recommend the review article from *Frontiers in Human Neuroscience* as a good starting point,[6] as well as Professor Edward Bullmore's excellent and thought-provoking book about mental health, *The Inflamed Mind*.[7]

Stress in real life

So far so statistical, theoretical, and evidence-based. It's a bit dry, all this talk of burdens of disease, life expectancy, pathways, and markers. What does it look like in a real life? Well, I can offer you mine and that of my family. I may be a generalist, professionally speaking, but in this particular field at least I am an expert.

As part of my GP training, I spent some time as a dermatologist. I was very lucky to work in a department that included some world leaders in their field. They were a very smart and compassionate bunch. My boss was firmly of the opinion that the more experience you had of disease, the better a doctor it made you. Now clearly there are some diseases you'd prefer not to experience, never mind attempt to acquire. However, now, after twenty years of clinical practice, I absolutely agree with him. He also used to tell his juniors that it was important to touch patients with skin conditions, reminding us that dermatology was 'a contact sport'. Actually, the whole of life is a contact sport and the more we experience the better we are able to get alongside, empathize with, and help others. Although I would not have chosen to experience the high levels of stress that we were exposed to for decades as a family, it has taught me a lot and is probably the reason that I'm writing this book today.

As a family we have faced the same sort of everyday challenges and background life-load that everyone does, but my son's severe and complex epilepsy provided us with some serious, next-level experience. Like the unfortunate, unsuspecting frog in the saucepan full of water that's slowly getting hotter, we tolerated gradually increasing levels of stress for quite a long time . . . or so we thought. The problem with stress-related illness is that it has a long lead-in time. The point at which you notice that the wheels are beginning to creak might be just before they actually fall off. The sustained levels of stress and the associated inflammatory response have been wreaking havoc behind the scenes. Our bodies are incredible in terms of the insult and injury they can recover from, but too much for too long eventually takes its toll and overcomes our capacity to restore and to heal.

In our case, the consequence of constant hypervigilance (since Luke required 24-hour care and could not be left unsupervised), sleep deprivation, and permanent low-level anxiety, punctuated by regular peaks of much more acute anxiety due to medical emergencies, manifested in a number of different ways. It affected all of us. My wife Beccy and I bore the brunt of it, as we did our best to shield our other children in an attempt to give them as normal a life as possible. During the days when I was at work, Beccy was the first on call. During the nights, it was my turn, as I found it easier to get back to sleep after dealing with one of Luke's seizures — or more likely, a cluster of them.

We were tired all the time. Our moods were up and down, sometimes low, often anxious and irritable. We didn't always have time to eat well or to be physically active. I drank more than was good for me. It was tempting to reach for the bottle when I got home after a tough day at work, knowing that I probably had a tough night ahead; one that might be spent lying on a mattress in Luke's room, heart pounding as I waited for the start of the next seizure. Our relationship was affected because we didn't feel able to look after ourselves, never mind each other. We were heads-down, nose to the grindstone, in survival mode. We lived like this for twelve years, with the last seven or so being particularly intense as Luke entered adolescence and his seizures became worse, more frequent, and life-threatening.

Of course, there were lots of good things in our lives. We had good friends, my job was secure, and we were part of a church community – although the latter could be a double-edged sword, with people's response to our situation ranging from kind and practical support, through to awkward silence and even occasional ham-fisted and hurtful attempts to theologize our troubles away. We have had a lot of happy times and rewarding experiences as a family, particularly seeing Luke's brothers grow up as close-knit and caring individuals, with compassion and faith, who have a much more rounded view of the world and a wider perspective than many of their friends around them in comfortable, narrowly focused, middle-class suburbia. I believe that growing up as Luke's brothers and carers has made them better human beings, particularly as Luke leads by example in always caring for others, despite his significant personal challenges.

It is fair to say, however, that despite all of the good things in our lives, the wheels were creaking and eventually they fell off. We couldn't just carry on in survival mode, because we were in danger of not actually surviving, either as individuals or as a family. We had to take stock of our lives and make some changes, for all of our sakes. Beccy and I needed to look after ourselves better so that we could look after each other and our kids. Friends stepped up to help us with day-to-day practicalities, such as childcare and the school run. I was signed off work for a while so I could focus on our family, and Beccy had some time away to rest and recuperate. The National Health Service offered the usual options of psychological support and medication. All of these things were short-term measures that gave us breathing space while we did some thinking about the long term.

As I have already disclosed, towards the end of Luke's time living at home with us, I was diagnosed with inflammatory bowel disease; a potentially serious and lifelong condition. In the most severe cases it can result in major surgery, frequent hospital visits, and debilitating, restricting, long-term symptoms. I had to use medication every day to bring the symptoms under control and required regular blood tests to monitor it. The specialist nurse and consultant involved in my care were very nice people, but the only tools they had in their box were those of conventional, disease-based medicine. Their advice was helpful in the short term, the medication essential to bring some of my symptoms under control. They didn't ask questions about my life and the background to my presentation. They didn't look at the bigger picture or encourage me to do so.

I had to look after myself better if I was to be in a fit state to fulfil my personal and professional responsibilities. This was the start of my looking into what it meant to truly feel well, born not out of intellectual curiosity, but driven by necessity. I needed to be in a good place if I was to be a good doctor, husband, father, and friend. Beccy recognized that she had areas she needed to work on too. There was some work we had to do together – it is well documented that there is a higher divorce rate between couples who have a child with special needs.

Fast-forward to today and we are all in a much better place. The things we have done are mostly pretty simple, which of course is not necessarily the same as easy. Spoiler alert – there has not been a silver bullet. Some things have worked and stuck, others have not. I would say that key areas have been: better communication (helped by relationship counselling); more regular physical activity both in home and work settings; prioritizing sleep more (a big one for me); developing mindfulness (meditation and writing for me, painting and sewing for Beccy); eating better (a lower-carbohydrate, less inflammatory diet); and doing more planning, so that all of these important things (including spending time with our friends, as well as each other) can happen. Discussing our priorities and what we would like to happen means that we are more likely both to do more of what we need, and less of what we don't. We have recognized that our capacity to do life is finite and so if there are things we want to add in, then we have to get rid of other things that aren't beneficial to us.

Now you might be feeling a little cheated, as I've just rattled through what worked for us in one measly paragraph. Never fear. At the end of this chapter, I will illustrate some of my prescribed suggestions for a renewed mind with some of these personal details. After all, I want to show you, not just tell you. Before we get onto that, we need to talk about rest.

Hurry up and rest

Although I could have simply made 'resting' one of my tips for lowering stress and enjoying better mental health, it's a topic which deserves much more detail than being a bullet point.

Rest is not something that is a nice-to-have option, a luxury that we may be fortunate enough to add to our daily routine if we have the time and the space in our diary. It's not an optional extra. It's fundamental to our wellbeing and something that we should actively pursue.

Rest has been important to us as an evolving species. As I've already mentioned, when we were hunter-gatherers, we didn't work a 9–5 day. We had periods of more intense activity, followed by periods of rest. We operated like this up until about 10,000 years ago, which is more or less a blink of the eye in evolutionary terms. Our bodies still require rest in the same way that they require movement. They haven't yet learnt to cope with our species' unfortunate tendency in the last 50–100 years to eliminate rest as much as possible. Even if such adaptation were both possible and desirable, it's not going to happen in our lifetime. The elimination of rest is another example of counterintuitive decision-making, creating a toxic environment of busy-ness, which we have managed somehow to turn into a virtue. We should remember that we are not machines. Even if we were, we would still need our batteries recharging.

In case you are confusing rest with idleness, rest doesn't mean doing nothing. The decision to rest can be an intentional, active one. Rest is not the opposite of work, rather it can be its partner. Even as late as the second part of last century it was assumed that when resting, the brain went offline and did very little. However, we now know this not to be true. Our brain uses about 20% of the energy we expend each day just staying alive, including during rest periods. Almost 100 years ago, the measurement of the electrical activity of the brain (using a device called an electroencephalogram) in resting subjects suggested that there was still a lot going on, and this has subsequently been confirmed by functional MRI scanning. We now understand the concept of the default mode network (DMN), which is one of the resting circuits of our brain and fires up when we are having downtime. When we are resting, when we allow our minds to wander and daydream, the DMN springs to life and is vital for learning, memory, reflection, making sense of the world, creativity, and problem-solving. Ever struggled with a problem, unable to solve it despite furious focus, and then eventually given up . . . only for inspiration to strike you when you're in the shower? That's the DMN in action. Tim Kreider wrote in *The New York Times*:

The space and quiet that idleness provides is a necessary condition for standing back from life and seeing it whole, for making unexpected connections and waiting for the wild summer lightning strikes of inspiration – it is, paradoxically, necessary to getting any work done.[8]

It all goes back to environment, to default settings. Where is the historical evidence from the randomized controlled trials and meta-analyses, which society has considered carefully in constructing the modern working week? When was it proved that work martyrdom and not taking holidays makes individuals more productive and companies perform better? John Pencavel, a British Professor of Economics at Stanford University, looked at this in his discussion paper on working hours and productivity, using data from munitions workers in the Second World War.[9] After fifty hours, productivity dropped off a cliff. Increasing working hours from 56 to 70 hours per week did not produce any significant additional output. That's over half a day a week that could have been spent doing something else other than work, at no cost to the employer but possibly of great benefit to the employee. He argued against seven-day working, showing that that the absence of a rest day damages output.

You might be wondering whether we can apply data from female factory workers in the middle of a war over seventy years ago to today's workplace. I believe that this is even more relevant to modern-day working practices based in offices or our homes, often staring at a screen and having to use our intellect much more than we would to assemble parts on a factory floor.

In his book, *The Seven Habits of Highly Effective People*, Dr Stephen Covey writes: 'We must never become too busy sawing to take time to sharpen the saw.'[10]

It's important that you protect and develop your most precious resource – which is you. Not resting is bad for you and bad for business. If you would like to spend some more time reading and thinking about this very important subject, I heartily recommend to you John Mark Comer's *The Ruthless Elimination of Hurry*, a beautiful and challenging book.[11] Reading it changed my life. I hope that in devoting just a few paragraphs to this subject I have conveyed my urgent message to you – that we need to hurry up and rest.

Rediscovering mindfulness

We can't consider the importance of rest without considering mindfulness. This has become something of a buzzword in the recent past. Even in just the last few years we have seen both a heavy promotion of it and a backlash against it: modern-day, mental-wellbeing Marmite. Advocates see it as the great panacea to all the woes of modern living, something all children should learn in school. Others see the opportunity presented by McMindfulness, with a market worth billions. Sceptics describe it as another symptom of self-absorption and, in the worst case, a tool used cynically by big business to keep corporate slaves productive and accepting of their working conditions and fate. So, what is it? Where does it come from? Does it work, and if so, how might we apply it? Here's my simple guide to mindfulness:

Mindfulness is nothing new

Mindfulness is the basic human ability to be fully present in the moment, aware of what is going on inside and outside ourselves, without judging or reacting to it. It is usually achieved through the core practice of meditation, so the two terms are often used interchangeably. If I were to differentiate, I would say that mindfulness is the end result of the process rather than the tools used to develop it, but let's not nit pick.

The practice of mindfulness has been documented over thousands of years. It is often said that the roots are in Buddhism, but we also see them in Judaism, Islam, and Christianity. In fact, meditation is mentioned in the book of

Genesis, almost 2,000 years before the birth of Christ. 'Lectio Divina' is an example of a Christian mindfulness tradition, a contemplative way of reading the scriptures combined with meditation and prayer.

Mindfulness was embraced more in the secular Western world towards the end of last century. Jon Zabat-Kinn was a particularly important figure in this respect, fusing Eastern tradition with Western science in the 1970s to produce therapy for his clients. Although the basic principles of mindfulness practice are universal, mindfulness can be characterized crudely as a *horizontal* relationship in the secular world, focusing on ourselves and our relationships with others, and a more *vertical* one in a Christian context, between ourselves and God. Actually there's quite a lot of overlap and I think it's artificial to separate them entirely.

Mindfulness is not woo-woo

There is a solid and growing evidence base for the effect of mindfulness to treat both mental and physical disorders. Mindfulness-Based Stress Reduction (MBSR) and Mindfulness-Based Cognitive Therapy (MBCT) are validated therapeutic tools used by psychologists in treating people with mental-health problems, including depression and anxiety.

Do you remember me describing inflammation as a possible common soil for many different diseases, and it being possible to measure raised inflammatory markers in both physical and mental health conditions that may be stress-related? Mindfulness has been shown to reduce these inflammatory biomarkers in people with cognitive impairment,[12] and inflammatory bowel disease,[13] among other conditions. Furthermore, structural and functional changes in the brain, including regions associated with the default mode network I referred to earlier in this chapter, have been demonstrated as a result of mindfulness training, and even more exciting than just measuring levels of things in the blood, this has been associated with improved depression scores.[14] This is possibly owing to the plasticity of our brains, which continue to produce new nerve cells every day into adulthood – a process known as neurogenesis. Concerns have been expressed that mindfulness encourages selfishness, but there is evidence to show that it causes increased levels of altruism.[15]

Mindfulness is for the many, not the few

Not only should mindfulness not been seen as woo-woo, it should also not be considered an optional add-on or plug-in for those that have the luxury of affording it. The practice of mindfulness addresses a deficit that has been created by our environment and culture, restoring what we have been robbed of, whether by ourselves or by others. A life fully lived is by definition a mindful one. That's not to say that everyone consciously practises meditation every day, although I think this would help most of us. You may do this instinctively, not fully aware of what you are doing. Your mindful activity might be reading a book, listening to your favourite music, going for a walk, painting, running, doing archery, or even online gaming. These activities require focus and reduce the likelihood of you being distracted by your thoughts and the outside world.

I have read articles by newspaper columnists chronicling – gleefully in some cases – their failed attempts to develop a mindfulness practice. We should remember that developing any skill requires practice. One session of mindfulness isn't going to change your life. It's not a quick fix. The more regularly you do it, the better you get at it and the more you benefit from it. You can't run a marathon if you've never even run to the end of the road. You shouldn't expect to hit the middle of a target every time you release the arrow.

I also understand the concern that the practice of mindfulness might open up a can of worms for some and even lead to a worsening of mental health problems. I have not been able to find any good-quality evidence for this in the medical literature. One size does not fit all. There are different approaches to developing a mindfulness practice and if one form doesn't suit you, you can always consider other approaches, perhaps with support from a mental health professional if need be. The important thing is to find something that works for you and to avoid ending up being stressed about not being good at mindfulness, while looking guiltily at the unused apps on your phone!

My experience of mindfulness

Developing a mindfulness practice was at the top of my to-do list when things were at their most challenging at home. I had always compartmentalized life into boxes, which was protective to some degree and helped me cope for longer than I might have done otherwise. Despite this, I was aware that I was finding it hard to switch out of fight-or-flight mode, whether at home with my family or at work with my patients and colleagues. I'm an avid consumer of podcasts and after listening to an interview with Andy Puddicombe, a former Buddhist monk and the founder of *Headspace*, I downloaded the app onto my phone. I started small, just five minutes a day, and gradually worked my way through the different modules that were on offer. I did this consistently for the next 18 months or so, managing to meditate most days. Although you will probably get the best idea of what mindfulness meditation typically involves by watching a video or listening to an audio guide, you might like to try the following exercise:

- Find a quiet space where you are unlikely to be disturbed for five minutes. Set a timer if you wish.

- Sit quietly in an upright, relaxed posture. It doesn't matter exactly how you sit, but it should be comfortable and most people will find it helpful to have their arms resting on their lap.

- Notice the sensation of your chest rising and falling as you breathe in and out in your natural rhythm.

- Take a deep breath in, filling your lungs (ideally through your nose), hold it for a second or two, then breathe out slowly through pursed lips. You will notice that exhaling this way takes longer and that your heart rate slows as you do it. Repeat this pattern four or five times before allowing your breathing to settle into a normal rhythm again.

- Scan your body from your head down to your toes, noting how you feel physically, without dwelling on or worrying about any particular sensations, but just acknowledging them.

- Notice how you feel mentally and emotionally today. Some people find it helpful to give themselves a score from 1 to 10. Again, do this without judging the result. It's just an observation.

- Notice your surroundings: what you can see, hear, feel, smell, or touch? Include the feeling of the chair or floor against your back, bottom, and legs. How do your arms feel resting on the chair or in your lap? Spend a few seconds on each sense.

- Take a moment to reflect on why you are doing this. Is it to feel calmer, to improve focus, to improve your relationships with others or God? A different thing might spring to mind depending on the situation.

- Now close your eyes and continue by noting the feeling in your chest as it rises and falls, your breath as it goes in and out, not trying to alter your pattern of breathing, just observing it. Don't worry about 'emptying your mind'. Thoughts may come into your head. That's okay. Instead of dwelling on them, allow them to pass by like leaves in a stream. Continue to focus on your breathing. Do this for a few minutes or until your timer goes off.

- Finish your meditation gradually rather than stopping suddenly. Take note again of your physical and mental state, and your surroundings. Open your eyes. Take a few seconds to adjust before getting up and walking around rather than leaping straight into action. If you can, stay in this relaxed state of mind for a while as you get on with the rest of your day.

How do you feel? Relaxed? Calm? More peaceful?

There's good and bad news about what happens next. The bad news is that mindfulness is not magic. You aren't going to be able to feel like this 24 hours a day, floating along in a Zen kind of way. Your life, and the load that goes with it, is still where you left it. Don't be discouraged. The good news is that mindfulness is contagious, spreading out to affect the whole of your life and maybe even the lives of others. There's a fascinating clip on YouTube of how just one tablespoon of olive oil can spread out across a large body of water and have a calming effect on the waves around it.[16] Mindfulness can have the same effect. With repeated practice I have noticed that it has changed how I do everyday things whether it be showering, walking, driving, eating, reading emails, getting my work done, interacting with others, reading the Bible, or praying. You can't help it. You don't need to chase after it, it just happens.

What can we learn about stress and mindset from the Bible?

Stress is part of life.

> Consider it pure joy, my brothers and sisters, whenever you face trials of many kinds, because you know that the testing of your faith produces perseverance. Let

> perseverance finish its work so that you may be mature
> and complete, not lacking anything. (James 1: 2–4, NIV)

Stress is an inevitable consequence of living. Instead of spending all our energies on the impossible task of trying to avoid it (which is innately and therefore ironically stressful), we should acknowledge it, learn from it, and so be better able to manage our response to it. You can't become resilient without experiencing struggle. If anyone ever tries to sell you the path to a stress-free existence, you may wish to buy some of their stock of snake oil and horse manure at the same time. The preaching of a prosperity doctrine – the idea that if you are good enough then good things will happen to you and conversely, that bad things only happen to bad people – is misguided and ignorant. Stress is inevitable, a chronic stress response is not. Your faith doesn't make you immune to the slings and arrows that life throws at you; it determines how you deal with them. My sister-in-law once posted a quote on Facebook, which said: 'I will stop looking for calmer waters and accept the fact that we were made for the waves.'

Worrying is pointless

> Therefore do not worry about tomorrow, for tomorrow
> will worry about itself. Each day has enough trouble of
> its own. (Matthew 6: 34, NIV)

> And which of you by being anxious can add a single
> hour to his span of life? (Matthew 6: 27, ESV)

Wise words from Jesus himself. It makes sense to be mindful of circumstances that we can control, and to take the action needed to improve a situation or to avoid disaster. I'm not suggesting we should all stick our heads in the sand when a bill needs to be paid or a deadline needs to be met. However, worrying about things that are out of your control will not increase your lifespan or healthspan but, as you now know from reading this chapter, it may well shorten it.

Beware of the evil twins

> And I saw that all toil and all achievement spring from one person's envy of another. This too is meaningless, a chasing after the wind. Fools fold their hands and ruin themselves. Better one handful with tranquillity than two handfuls with toil and chasing after the wind.
> (Ecclesiastes 4: 4–6, NIV)

Remember the malevolent siblings, Comparison and Expectation? The ones that rob us of our joy, make us jealous, and leave us striving permanently to achieve and acquire? There's nothing wrong with a bit of aspiration, but we should always stop to ask ourselves why we are doing what we are doing and what our end goal is. Will it make us happier? Will it make others happier?

Our relationship with God is a source of strength

> I sought the Lord, and he answered me and delivered me from all my fears. (Psalm 34: 4, ESV)

Do not be anxious about anything, but in every situation, by prayer and petition, with thanksgiving, present your requests to God. And the peace of God, which transcends all understanding, will guard your hearts and your minds in Christ Jesus. (Philippians 4: 6f, NIV)

When it comes to being resilient, our relationships are vital and none more so than our relationship with creator, redeemer, and friend. Just before I started my first job as a (frankly terrified) junior doctor, my mother gave me a verse: 'I can do all things through him who strengthens me' (Philippians 4: 13).

When the crash-bleep went off in the middle of a night on call, I would sprint towards the location where someone had just suffered a cardiac arrest, white coat and stethoscope flapping as I ran, feet pounding the corridor almost as loudly as my heart pounded in my ears, uttering this as a mantra between gasping breaths. In a weekend on call where I might sleep for three or four hours in seventy-two, I needed every available resource and certainly wasn't going to turn down a helping hand from the Almighty. Prayer is the cornerstone of how you build your relationship with God.

Rest and wait for the still, small voice

By waiting and calm you shall be saved, in quiet and trust lies your strength. (Isaiah 30: 15, NABRE)

He makes me lie down in green pastures. He leads me beside still waters. (Psalm 23: 2, ESV)

Come to me, all you who are weary and burdened, and I will give you rest. Take my yoke upon you and learn from me, for I am gentle and humble in heart, and you will find rest for your souls. For my yoke is easy and my burden is light. (Matthew 11: 28–30, NIV)

God is rest. When he created the world, he saw that what he had done was good, and he rested. Jesus prioritized rest and prayer in his time on earth, no matter how demanding the crowd got, or how urgent the situation. He knew that this was what he needed to be strong enough to do his Father's will. He went to quiet places. He spent time alone. He prayed. He spent time with his friends. He knew, several millennia before data would be available about how working hours affected productivity, that we all need a regular time of rest, a Sabbath: prioritized and protected time set aside purely for resting. It doesn't matter so much *when* you do it, or *how* you do it, just that you *do* it.

In the Old Testament we have the story of Elijah, one of God's most awesome prophets. He was major league, a real heavy hitter and not to be trifled with. According to biblical accounts he raised the dead, stopped it raining for over three years, and went toe to toe with the evil King Ahab and Queen Jezebel (cue lots of booing), while taking on all the prophets of the false god, Baal (and now some hissing). It all came to a head in a face-off between with him and a mere 450 prophets of Baal on top of Mount Carmel. I don't want to spoil the story for you if you haven't read it, but it doesn't end well for the prophets of Baal.

Realizing he was in deep trouble with the king and queen, he decided to make himself scarce and fled into the wilderness.

God told Elijah to expect him. There followed a series of cataclysmic events (a storm, an earthquake, and a fire). Elijah, like you or me, might have been forgiven for assuming this was how God would reveal himself. But he wasn't in any of those. In the end, it was through a still, small voice. That's how God speaks to most of us. To quote A.J. Sherrill in his excellent book *Quiet: Hearing God Amidst the Noise*:

> **Prayer must become more for us than thinking thoughts and saying words to God. We simply run out of things to say. At some point our relationship with God demands we move away from words, away from noise and away from the mental chatter toward discovering God in the quiet, the stillness and the silence.[17]**

What is your culture?

Consider your church, community group, or organization. What's the mindset *about* mindset? Are you conforming to the likeness of this world, sucked into the fast lane like everyone else? How's your digital hygiene? Are you competing with, and comparing yourselves to, each other, or another church, or diocese?

What sort of conversations do you have about stress? Is it worn as a badge of honour amongst the leadership? Do people have the opportunity to open up about how they are feeling? Do you have work martyrs in your team? Are you one of them? Have you been complicit in encouraging this culture? When do you send emails? When do you expect people to reply to them?

What is the example set by the leadership? Is it an authentic, credible one?

How do you give each other space, ensuring that you have enough margin in your lives personally and professionally? How does your organization plan holidays, rest days, and the pattern of the working week? If Sunday is a work day for you, when is your Sabbath?

What emphasis do you put on mental health, compared to spiritual or physical health? Are you still trying to separate these from each other? What mental health resources are available to your congregation and team members, internally or externally? Do you practise what you preach as a leader? Remember the safety demonstration on every plane flight when you are reminded that when oxygen masks drop from the ceiling you should put your own on first before attempting to help others.

My prescription for enjoying a renewed mind

For individuals

1. Remember that wellbeing means being well in body, mind and soul

When considering your mind, don't forget your body. Getting enough sleep, being physically active, and eating well are vital for your mental health, at least as effective as medication for most of us. Exercise reduces depression and may be as good as cognitive behavioural therapy.[18] Adopting a Mediterranean diet has been shown to improve moderate to severe depression in over 30 per cent of subjects, with only four people needing treatment for one to fully recover.[19] Pharmaceutical companies would kill to be able to quote such stats for their products. The most powerful tool for mental health is prevention. What you eat and how much you move is part of the toolkit.

2. Don't view stress as inherently good or bad

Your response to it is what matters. Consider describing it as something else, whether to yourself or others, with fewer negative connotations, such as life-load. How you frame it can make a difference. There's also difference between a stress reaction (occurring immediately and often automatically in response to an external factor in the moment) and a stress response (how you are mindful of it, process it internally, and make choices about how you think and behave as a result). You can't control what other people do. If you are triggered by something or someone, consider it an opportunity for self-examination and try to find a better way to react to it.

3. Practise gratitude

No matter how difficult your circumstances, I'm willing to bet that you can find three things each day that you are grateful for. It could be anything: the sun in the sky, the air that you breathe, the place that you live, the freedoms that you enjoy, your job, the people in your life, your faith. There is evidence that people who do this enjoy better mental health as a result, with associated changes in the brain demonstrated by functional MRI scanning.[20]

Life can often feel as if you are running into a headwind, but the reality for most of us is that we have a lot of tailwinds behind us too, which we forget about and take for granted. Naming a few of these things is a good way to start each day.

4. Connect with nature

One of the consequences of our increasingly busy lives, particularly in urban environments, is that we may suffer from nature deficiency. It is generally accepted these days that being outside in nature has many health benefits, whether these are due simply to addressing the deficiency or having additional benefits on top. The Japanese use the term 'forest bathing' and have even developed the speciality of Forest Medicine out of this. Forest bathing has been shown to increase both the levels of white blood cells (important for fighting infection) and anti-cancer proteins. Reductions in blood pressure, heart rate, and levels of stress hormones have also been demonstrated, as well as improved scores for depression, anxiety, and fatigue.[21] Like movement, there may be an ideal dose beyond which there is no extra measurable benefit, other than enjoying the experience. One study suggests that up to two hours a week of exposure to nature promotes wellbeing.[22]

Don't worry if you don't have a forest nearby. Exposure to nature takes many forms including gardening, farming, conservation work, walking, and cycling in green spaces. MIND, a mental health organization in the UK, use the term 'ecotherapy' to describe these activities, which I really like. People can sign up for the available schemes or be referred by health professionals. We are all aware of the National Health Service, but let's be mindful of the benefits offered by the *natural* health service.

5. Relationships: Nurturing, pruning and weeding

Relationships are a key determinant of wellbeing. I will be going into this in more detail in Chapter 9. For now, I would encourage you simply to think of the relationships in your life like the plants in a garden. You may wish to sow seeds in some areas, striking up new relationships with people that you feel will enhance your life (and hopefully you theirs!). Think about investing in the relationships that need feeding and nurturing so they can blossom and grow. Some might need a bit of pruning. Consider whether any of your relationships are more like weeds — ugly, blocking out the sunlight, and stopping others from growing. Choosing to end a toxic relationship is at least as important as seeking more positive ones.

6. Be realistic

Although it may be flattering to be asked to do something, and it feels good to be able to say 'yes' to your friend, family member, or boss, just remember that your resources are finite. You only have so much to give, a pool of energy that is shared between physical and mental capacity. Don't spread yourself too thin. It will only backfire and result in you disappointing others and yourself if you are unable to keep your word. Be honest with people and be prepared to say 'no', or at least 'not now'.

7. Maintain perspective and frame the future positively

In the midst of the Covid-19 pandemic, I have heard the wise words repeated over and over that this too will pass and we will meet again. It has always been the case, however hard it may be right now to see light at the end of the tunnel. Whatever you have been through, if you have learnt from your mistakes, developed new skills and different ways of thinking and become more resilient, then remind yourself of these positives. Sometimes it might just be congratulating yourself that you've made it through another day.

8. Focus on what you can control

I don't know about you, but there are plenty of things in my life to worry about; things that I am both in control of and responsible for. I definitely don't have time to waste ruminating on all the things that are entirely out of my control. Think of those thoughts like the leaves in the stream that I mentioned when describing a meditation exercise. Observe them floating by, and then get on with your life. Practising mindfulness will help you with this. Speaking of which . . .

9. Develop your mindfulness muscles

You could start with the exercise I have described. You may wish to look at some videos or read further. Personally, I recommend that you consider signing up for a course or use an app. These are more likely to help you form a new habit that sticks. Don't expect instant results. If you are aware that you are distracted when you are attempting to meditate, rather than getting frustrated view it as a sign that you are making progress. If you pray, make mindfulness part of your prayer life. I found it made prayer more meaningful for me and deepened my faith, because it stopped prayer from being a one-way street, with me just talking to God about my list of worries and requests until I had run out of things to say. I was getting really bored of the sound of my own voice. Now I feel that I'm resting, waiting, and listening more. I usually start writing sessions with five minutes of meditation and some prayer, which has really helped with focus, creativity, and my relationship with God.

10. Set up your own Sabbath

It doesn't matter whether you rest for a whole day, a half day, or a few hours here and there across the week. Think about what works for you. What can you realistically implement? What will you be able to stick to and have others respect? If you really believe you don't have any time to spare across the week, work out how many hours you spend watching Netflix and disappearing down the rabbit hole of social media, then get back to me. I don't need more hours in my day, I just need to use them better. Think about what *doing Sabbath* would mean for you or your family. Will you turn your phone off, or at least the notifications? Will you do it together? Will you use the time to develop your relationships with your family and with God?

11. Digital decluttering

As part of considering how you rest and practise the Sabbath, think about how you can get the best of out of technology instead of letting it get the best of you. If we are driven by FOMO, we end up unhappy and unfocused. Instead, take a minimalist approach by thinking about what you enjoy most in life. Use technology where it helps you with this. Discard it if it doesn't.

Forget multitasking. It's a myth, regardless of your gender. Constantly switching attention impairs brain function and stops you focusing and getting into the flow state that you need to be effective. Do one thing at a time. Plan your time and workflow accordingly. You might consider the principles of the

Pomodoro Technique, breaking work down into short focused intervals separated by planned breaks. I have 'Pomodoro playlists' of my favourite electronic and ambient music, each about 25 minutes long, to remind me when to stop, take breaks, and switch to doing something else.

Practise waiting. Don't check your phone when in the queue in the coffee shop or waiting to cross the road. Give yourself downtime and daydream so that you can rest. It will also allow your DMN to fire up and perhaps solve that tricky problem you've been stuck on. Your life should be intentional and this includes using social media: use it when you need to and for something that you want to do, rather than what someone else wants you to do.

Consider a full or partial digital detox. Think about what you could eliminate from your screen and your life. Turn off notifications on your phone (I promise you this will be a huge relief, once you've got over the short-lived period of post-notification FOMO). Uninstall some of your apps (turning your smartphone into a *dumb*-phone), or at least move them to a folder away from your phone's home page. Consider making a part of your day or a day of your week device-free, putting your phone or tablet away, or even in a box (along with those of your family members if you can persuade them, as it will work better if you do it together). Use out-of-office settings to let people know when you will next read and respond to their email. Set a time limit for how much you can use certain apps on your devices each day. You can configure your wireless router to limit Wi-Fi access at particular times for specific devices, whether they belong to you or your kids. Don't have your phone in your bedroom at night.

If this all sounds a bit scary and you don't want to go cold-turkey then just pick one or two and scale your plan up or down depending on how things are going. If you want to explore this topic more deeply, I recommend Cal Newport's excellent *Digital Minimalism*.[23] Humans and technology have always had a master–slave relationship. Let's keep it the right way around.

12. *Be kind to yourself*

Partly because you deserve it and partly because unless you do, you can't be kind to other people. The tougher your situation, the more aware you are of the changes you need to make, the more overwhelmed you may feel. That's okay – it's natural to feel like this. There may be things in your life that you can't change, things which are historical facts. Each one is just a risk factor, nothing more. If you can't change them, you can mitigate them by developing new protective factors into your life. You don't need to be anxious about anxiety, stressed about stress. Just take a simple first step. It might be a change in what you eat, how much you move, or how much sleep you get. It could be addressing a relationship at home or at work. It may involve turning off the notifications on your phone or uninstalling some applications. It might be starting with five minutes a day of protected time for you to meditate or pray, or even just to rest.

You don't need to be perfect seven days a week. Even one day a week is better than none. You will have setbacks. Some things will work, some things will not. When this happens you can view this not as a personal failure, but as a failure of the system you set up. Don't give up. You can learn from this, try again, and succeed.

For organizations

1. Lead by personal example

Based on my unscientific sampling, the default setting of most people I know who are in positions of leadership is 'stressed to the eyeballs'. There is an obvious discordance between what they preach from the pulpit and what they practise in their personal lives. I once monitored the blood pressure of a patient of mine who was a vicar: it was pretty good some of the time, but there were some very concerning spikes in his readings throughout the day. When we analysed the data, they coincided exactly with church meetings. He was a very kind man who had great difficulty saying no to anything, struggled to delegate, and worked long hours. He lived on the church premises, which didn't help him with his boundary issues.

As a leader you may feel that you have to be seen to be first into work and last out, sacrificing yourself on the altar of service. The implication, the unspoken assumption, is that this approach is both necessary and a virtue. As you now know, it is most emphatically not either. If Olympic athletes can only perform at their peak for a few hours a day at most before eventually suffering burnout, it's highly unlikely that you will do better. Remember that and ask yourself whether it's really necessary to make that phone call or send that email at silly o'clock. It's natural to feel responsible as a leader or owner of a company but remember the oxygen-mask analogy. The best thing that you can do to help others enjoy a renewed mind is to develop one yourself.

2. Set the culture

Share your challenges and frailties with others. Being open will encourage others in your organization to be open too. You might be worried about what will happen if you listen to people and give them the chance to open up. I'll tell you what will happen: you will have a workforce which is finally able to be honest about the issues it is struggling with and which, if it can then be helped to start addressing some of them, will become much more fulfilled and productive as a result. Don't preach perfection, individually or collectively. This will avoid you suffering inevitable disappointment.

We can't be good at everything. It's statistically very unlikely we will be even just average at everything. We have areas of strength and weakness. Our resources are finite. Decide what you want to focus on. Being exceptional in some areas requires acceptance of imperfection in others. Having the right balance of people and skillsets in a team is the recipe for success.

3. Build rest into work

Make sure that everyone takes the annual leave they are entitled to. Consider the implications of shorter, more frequent periods of leave. This might require more engineering of the working week to manage, but if people are happier and more productive it will be worth it. Likewise, look at the working week itself. Do you need everyone in the office or at their computer screens 9–5, five or six days a week? Companies are increasingly offering roles that can be done remotely from home, not even necessarily on the same continent. Offering more flexible working in terms of location, start, finish, and break times might result in improved performance, and higher levels of satisfaction and loyalty among the workforce. If word gets out, you will find it a lot easier to recruit as a result.

Some larger companies have nap rooms. If this isn't practical, at least encourage people to take proper breaks away from their desk, preferably getting outside in the fresh air. I go for a walk into town at lunchtime almost without fail, no matter how busy the day at the surgery. I figure that if I'm in the surgery from roughly 8 a.m. to 7 p.m. then having 20 or 30 minutes for lunch is not unreasonable. I also go for short walks around the building in between consultations and use the excuse of making a cup of tea to chat to my colleagues. Consider regular slots for yoga or meditation in the working week, and treat them with the same importance as you would a meeting. How can you use your physical workspace to help promote rest?

4. Don't honour work martyrs

The next time you are tempted to make such martyrdom a virtue, don't. Don't reward people for doing it. Consider it as dumb and inefficient rather than smart and heroic. I'm not suggesting public ridicule, but maybe a quiet word in someone's ear during an appraisal. You'll be doing a favour both to the individual and to the business by avoiding the wheels falling off, which would otherwise inevitably occur, with the resulting costs outweighing any previously imagined gains. If you're a leader, don't be a martyr yourself.

5. Develop a digital wellbeing policy

Have a clear understanding, even a written policy, about working hours, particularly when it comes to making calls, sending or responding to emails. Of course, there will be occasions where an urgent response is needed. Just as doctors define criteria for making a diagnosis, give some thought to, and describe for your team, what sort of scenarios these might be and have a clear plan for how to respond in that situation, making sure everyone understands what is required of them.

Check every now and then whether people are playing by the rules, or whether the rules need changing. Consider an outright ban on social media in the workplace, unless on a break. It will improve focus and therefore productivity, while potentially benefitting people's mental health for all the reasons I have already outlined. Engage your team in these decisions where appropriate. Ask them for their help in drawing up the codes of conduct, or at least take time to discuss the basis for these decisions with them, which in turn means people are more likely to stick to them.

Taking mental health seriously

Throughout the whole of this chapter, and indeed the whole of this book, I have referred frequently to the challenges and causes of, and potential therapeutic approaches to, mental-health problems. I haven't broken this chapter down into detailed sections on different mental health conditions. I'm not a psychiatrist and this isn't my specialist subject. Instead, I have looked at some of the common origins of both physical and mental illness.

Clearly everyone is different and one size does not fit all. When it comes to serious mental illness, such as bipolar affective disorder, schizophrenia, or major depression, a person may have a strong family history of such problems, loading the dice genetically before environment ever comes into play. I have yet to meet anyone who has sailed through life without any challenges to their mental wellbeing. Many will be able to improve and maintain it by simple measures like the ones I have recommend in this book.

As a society I do believe that we over-medicalize life, over-diagnose disease, and find it easier to prescribe a pill than to look deeper for the answers. I once heard a psychiatrist say that when people consult a doctor about a mental health problem, it is usually on one of the worst days of their life. Given time and perspective, however, many 'diagnoses' will evaporate. That said, some people do genuinely need more support from their doctors and mental health professionals, including the appropriate use of medication in severe illness. If you are such a person, or worried that you might be, please do seek medical advice. I'm not suggesting that anyone throw away their pills without consulting their doctor. I do believe that, whatever our situation may be, we can all take simple and small steps towards improved mental wellbeing and a renewed mind.

Notes

1. World Health Organization, 'Global, Regional, and National Disability-adjusted Life-Years (DALYs) for 333 Diseases and Injuries and Healthy Life Expectancy (HALE) for 195 Countries and Territories, 1990–2016: A Systemic Analysis for the Global Burden of Disease Study 2015'. Available at: https://www.thelancet.com/journals/lancet/article/PIIS0140-6736(17)32130-X/fulltext.

2. Manel Baucells and Rakesh Sarin, *Engineering Happiness: A New Approach for Building a Joyful Life* (University of California Press, 2012).

3. J.J. Chiang, N.A. Turiano, D.K. Mroczek, and G.E. Miller, 'Affective Reactivity to Daily Stress and 20-year Mortality Risk in Adults with Chronic Illness: Findings

from the National Study of Daily Experiences', *Health Psychology*, 37: 2 (2018), 170–178.

4. S. Meier, M. Mattheisen, O. Mors, P. Mortensen, T. Laursen, and B. Penninx, 'Increased Mortality among People with Anxiety Disorders: Total Population Study', *British Journal of Psychiatry*, 209: 3 (2016), 216–221.

5. T. Härkänen, K. Kuulasmaa, L. Sares-Jäske, et al., 'Estimating Expected Life-years and Risk Factor Associations with Mortality in Finland: Cohort study', *British Medical Journal Open*, 10 (2020), e033741.

6. Y-Z. Liu, Y-X. Wang. and C-L Jiang, 'Inflammation: The Common Pathway of Stress-related Diseases', *Frontiers in Human Neuroscience*, 11 (2017), 316.

7. Edward Bullmore, *The Inflamed Mind: A Radical New Approach to Depression* (Short Books, 2018).

8. Tim Krieder, 'The Busy Trap', *New York Times*, 30 June 2012. Available at: https://opinionator.blogs.nytimes.com/2012/06/30/the-busy-trap.

9. J. Pencavel, 'The Productivity of Working Hours', Discussion paper No. 8129, April 2014. Stanford University and IZA. Available at: http://ftp.iza.org/dp8129.pdf.

10. Stephen R. Covey, *The Seven Habits of Highly Effective People: Restoring the Character Ethic* (New York: Free Press, 2004).

11. John Mark Comer, *The Ruthless Elimination of Hurry: How to Stay Emotionally Healthy and Spiritually Alive in the Chaos of the Modern World* (Hodder & Stoughton, 2019).

12. T.K.S. Ng, J. Fam, L. Feng, et al., 'Mindfulness Improves Inflammatory Biomarker Levels in Older Adults with Mild Cognitive Impairment: A Randomized Controlled Trial', *Transatlantic Psychiatry* 10 (2020), 21.

13. R. González-Moret, A. Cebolla, X. Cortés, *et al.*, 'The Effect of a Mindfulness-based Therapy on Different Biomarkers among Patients with Inflammatory Bowel Disease: A Randomised Controlled Trial', *Scientific Reports*, 10 (2020), 6071.

14. C. Yang, A. Barrós-Loscertales, M. Li, et al., 'Alterations in Brain Structure and Amplitude of Low-Frequency after 8 Weeks of Mindfulness Meditation Training in Meditation-naïve Subjects', *Scientific Reports*, 9 (2019), 10977.

15. S.K. Iwamoto, M. Alexander, M. Torres, et al., 'Mindfulness Meditation Activates Altruism' *Scientific Reports*, 10 (2020), 6511.

16. What the Physics?!, 'Crazy Lake Experiment', 21 January 2016. Available at: https://youtu.be/f2H418M3V6M

17. A.J. Sherrill, *Quiet: Hearing God Amidst the Noise* (CreateSpace, 2014).

18. J. Rimer, K. Dwan, D.A. Lawlor, *et al.*, 'Exercise for Depression', *Cochrane Database Systematic Reviews*, 7 (2012), CD004366.

19. F.N. Jacka, A. O'Neil, R. Opie, et al., 'A randomised controlled trial of dietary improvement for adults with major depression: The "SMILES" trial', *BMC Medicine*, 15, (2017), 23.

20. Y. Wong, J. Owen, N. T. Gabana, J. W. Brown, S. McInnis, P. Toth, and L. Gilman, 'Does Gratitude Writing Improve the Mental Health of Psychotherapy Clients? Evidence from a Randomized Controlled Trial', *Psychotherapy Research*, 28: 2 (2018), 92–202.

21. Q. Li, 'Effets des Forêts et des Bains de Forêt (Shinrin-Yoku) sur la Santé Humaine: Une Revue de la Littérature [Effect of Forest Bathing (Shinrin-Yoku) on Human Health: A Review of the Literature]. *Santé Publique*. S1 (HS) (2019), 135–143.

22. M.P., White, I. Alcock, J. Grellier, et al., 'Spending at least 120 Minutes a Week in Nature is Associated with Good Health and Wellbeing', *Scientific Reports*, 9 (2019), 7730.

23. Cal Newport, *Digital Minimalism: Choosing a Focused Life in a Noisy World* (New York: Penguin, 2019).

9. Connections

Fear not, for I am with you. (Isaiah 41: 10, ESV)

The importance of being connected

We are social animals. Humans have evolved living in tribes. Without the tribe we would never have survived to reproduce and so continue evolving. Connections with others are vital for us, not just to survive but also to thrive. This shouldn't come as a news to anyone. John Donne famously declared almost 400 years ago that 'no man is an island'. Whether we are introverts or extroverts, we all need connections with other people. Everyone is different and, therefore, so is the extent to which we need connection to live a satisfying and happy life. However, saying you don't need people is the same as someone with a small appetite declaring they don't need food, or a free-diver declaring they don't need air. Like sleep, movement, food, and other kinds of medicine, it's about getting the dose right.

In considering wellbeing, we shouldn't just look at the physical wellbeing, which you might crudely call 'health'. This only accounts for about 20 per cent of what makes us flourish and live satisfying lives. We need to consider the wider determinants of health. These include the social, emotional, and cultural wellbeing of not only the individual, but the whole community. A narrow focus on the individual is short-sighted and ultimately self-defeating when you realize that individual wellbeing is determined, to some degree, by that of others around you.

Of the 'Five Ways to Wellbeing' mentioned in health and social-care settings, what is the number one recommendation? Connecting with others. It's placed above movement, learning new skills, giving to others, and mindfulness. If you think about it, community and connectedness are essential for most if not all of the other four ways to wellbeing too.

In almost a quarter of a century of medical practice, twenty years of it as a GP, I am now convinced that how connected we feel to others is the single most important determinant of wellbeing. If I had to pick one area to focus on with my patients, to the exclusion of all others, it would be this. Getting this right may be more important than screening programmes, blood tests and X-rays, specialist referrals, and medication reviews. It may be more important than your blood-pressure readings or cholesterol levels. Of course, there are times when an individual needs urgent treatment for a serious condition, but I believe that if we got connection right across the population as a whole, the outcome would be much greater wellbeing for all, including what we think of as health.

Community is a place where we feel we belong and other people notice if we are struggling. We discover who we are in the company of others, in vulnerability and interdependency. Being in a group promotes reflection, allowing us to bounce ideas off each other, to both challenge and support each other. Solitary thinking, although it has its merits, can't do this.

I have already talked about the blue zones, which are specific areas of the world where people enjoy unusually long lifespan and healthspan. One of the features common to all the zones, which are spread out across the world, is a physically active life of inconvenience. Another common feature is that of community. They are close-knit, live among each other, knowing and being known all their lives. Everyone has a place and is a part of the group, whatever their age or circumstances. They are great examples of places where the default environment remains natural and intuitive, left in the factory settings that they came with rather than forcefully altered to produce an unnatural, counterintuitive one.

So if all of this is obvious, if we have learnt anything from history and evolution, then surely we would all be getting better and better at this? Government policy would thus promote a community-based approach to doing life, encouraging us to consider the wellbeing of those around us, and even those who are further away. Healthcare providers would understand the importance of connectedness and would focus on this in consultations with patients, particularly those with complex needs and mental health problems. We'd all get the big picture, and live our lives accordingly, right? Well, as I've said before when considering our current default environmental settings for sleep, movement, nutrition, and mental health, the one thing you can say about humans is that we are, unfortunately, nothing if not consistent.

This is how it feels to be lonely

Loneliness is how you feel when there is a mismatch between the quantity and quality of the relationships that you have, and those that you want. It's an individual experience. Our personal characteristics, the situations we find ourselves in at different times, and the norms and values of the societies we live in, are all different and between them this determines whether or not we feel lonely. Any of these factors can change over time. A resilient person in good health and enjoying strong support may face disaster without feeling lonely. A person with chronic mental health problems and inadequate support may feel very lonely in the face of the simple challenges of day-to-day life. Loneliness can be transient or chronic, social, emotional, or existential.

Loneliness isn't necessarily bad. In fact, it's an essential part of the human condition, fundamental to our being. It can be a source of creative energy, driving people to make changes, to challenge injustice, to look more deeply into life's meaning, and find new ways of living. Just like stress, we all need the right dose in our lives. Too little and we never have time to reflect and to grow; too much however can cause pain, depression, despair, and even death. Loneliness is also not the same as being alone, as long as we feel that we are part of a community and are loved.

Loneliness in society

In our society we are facing an epidemic of news headlines telling us that we are in in the middle of an epidemic of loneliness. If this were true it would probably boost sales of this book. Thankfully for society, if not for my publisher, this is not the case – yet. Despite the increasingly panicked tone of reports by well-meaning organizations, and even the appointment of a Minister for Loneliness by the UK Government in 2018, the stats have been relatively stable, until recently. In survey after survey, on average about 10–15 per cent of the population in the developed world report consistent feelings of loneliness. It doesn't seem to be obviously rising over time, although it is a little difficult to dig through all the data.

There are two peaks of loneliness in life: one in very old age (which I would imagine you were expecting); and one in young adults aged 18–25, which may surprise you. This second group is in fact the loneliest in our population. In middle age through to early old age, we appear to be less lonely, perhaps because we are more secure in longer lasting relationships, surrounded by our families, and more selective about the people that we connect with. The reason that reported loneliness rises again in later old age is thought to be due to the loss of a spouse and increasing ill-health.

And yet despite being bereaved, sick, frail, and elderly you are less likely to experience loneliness than when you are apparently in the prime of your life as a young adult. It's also worth noting that this increased risk of loneliness is only found in developed countries. So, although young people from these backgrounds would generally be considered, globally speaking, to have every possible advantage, this may be the exception when it comes to meaningful connections with others in the world around them.

Although we may not be in the middle of a loneliness epidemic right now, there are early warning signs which, as a society, we ignore at our collective peril. The latest UK dataset from the Office for National Statistics, which measures national wellbeing, shows that people are more likely to feel lonely and that they are less able to rely on a spouse, family member, or friend if they have a problem.[1] The ground is beginning to shift. We've all seen disaster movies where the first signs of impending catastrophe are ignored, whether it's the mass migration of birds, early ground tremors near a fault line, or the sea level dropping as the tide gets sucked out before the arrival of the tidal wave. So what might those early warning signs be?

The cult of the individual and the pursuit of personal freedom

One of the reasons that we are the dominant species on the planet is not because we are the biggest, fastest, or strongest, but because we are able to communicate with, and look after, each other. Our genes may be selfish, but humans are not. We have traditionally formed relationships which are long-lasting and strengthen our ties to each other, and to any children we might have. There must be an evolutionary advantage to this, compared to the much older behaviours of promiscuity and producing as many offspring as possible. Love has power over fear and gives us a secure base from which to explore the world, both as children and adults. Any unwitting attempts to undo this are likely to have serious consequences, even if they aren't immediately apparent. Consider the irony of the cult of the individual. As cults go, it really isn't very well thought out. It lacks the usual core benefit of cult membership; that is, living with and working alongside like-minded people, who share each other's values and support each other. By definition this is impossible. The wider the message spreads, the bigger the cult grows, and the sooner it will lead to its own destruction.

Idolizing personal freedom and pursuing this to extremes is dangerous because it may result in people leaving the very groups and relationships, whether at home or at work, that their happiness and the happiness of others depend upon. And all because of the philosophy increasingly pushed upon us that, as individuals, we deserve to be happy and that this can somehow be done in a vacuum with no interdependencies. This philosophy is promoted on television and social media, often by those that want to sell us things that they need us to believe we cannot be happy without. Selfishness is not just acceptable, it's promoted.

My wife and I recently watched a series of *Married at First Sight*. Couples who meet for the first time at the altar are matched beforehand by 'experts'. These self-proclaimed experts say this is to ensure compatibility. My rather more jaundiced view is that it's to ensure that maximum entertainment ensues. Putting aside the ridiculous premise, even then within the show there was one participant who, knowing the rules of engagement (i.e. that they were taking part in a televised experiment to see if they could make their marriage work), still decided to pursue someone from another marriage, rather than focusing on their own. Their justification? That they had to do what was right for them and that they deserved to be happy, no matter the consequences for others. What shocked me was not that they behaved in this way, but that they were unashamed to do so in public, justifying themselves on camera for the world to see, as if it were something that was not only their right but a virtue.

In Chapter 8, I described how disconnection is a significant cause of stress and unhappiness. Rather than simply repeating myself, I'm going to put it another way: interdependency is what allows us not just to survive but thrive. Did you know that most of the cells in your body are not actually you? There are roughly 30–100 trillion cells in your body, and just under half of them belong to what you think of as 'you'. Most of the cells and DNA in our bodies come from the microscopic organisms that colonize us, including bacteria, viruses, and fungi. The majority of these organisms live in our bowel, making up the gut microbiome, which I referred to in Chapter 6. The relationship between us and these tiny colonists is a symbiotic one, meaning that it is mutually beneficial. If you were somehow able to strip away all of these extra cells and their DNA, your body would not only cease to function, but it would also fall apart and you would no longer be 'you'. So it is when it comes to our relationships with others. We don't exist in a vacuum. You are not an isolated entity but are defined, in part, by the nature of your relationships. Good relationships are symbiotic. They aren't just helpful, they are essential. They make us what we are and they make life worth living.

Losing our religion

The decline of religion in almost all developed nations is well documented. Broadly speaking, religiosity is high in poorer countries that are still developing, and lower in developed, more affluent nations (the one outlier here is the United States, where it has been speculated that the widening gap between rich and poor, with over 50 million people without health insurance, has created conditions for many that are similar to those in parts of the developing world).

In the UK there has been a marked post-war decline in those declaring themselves to be followers of Christianity, our largest religion. It may be that it's more age- than cohort-related, with most of those declaring themselves to be religious being over 50 years of age, and most of those who are not religious being younger. Now from a humanist or atheist perspective this may be considered a great thing; a demonstration that once we are educated and affluent enough we can shake off the shackles of superstition, and no longer be dependent on a mythical being to help us make sense of and deal with life. This demonstrates an ignorance of the role of organized religion which has, for thousands of years, been the glue that has held society together.

Regardless of the specifics, faith gives us a consistent framework for understanding and conduct, creating rules for life. We all have them, whether religious or not, and whether we realize them or not. The advantage of religion is that it makes it easier to identify what these rules are and for large numbers of individuals to behave in a consistent way, holding each other to account and creating a stable society. Believing these laws to be divinely ordained and universal creates an extra layer of cohesion and stability. Considering the individual as sacred gives meaning to rules that might otherwise be considered arbitrary.

Secularists will point out that we have political and judicial systems that provide us with this framework, and that to live as a productive and decent member of society does not therefore require religious belief. Absolutely true. Nowadays. It should also be pointed out that many of the rules by which we live today have their origins in religion, and were formalized in times when the majority considered themselves to be religious and there was no division between Church and State.

Don't get me wrong. Organized religion has a lot to answer for. As someone once said to me, 'I don't mind God, it's his followers that I can't stand!' Over the millennia it has been something of a double-edged sword, sometimes literally, used to justify some pretty horrible behaviours. In the case of most religions, that's exactly what it is – justification. We humans do an excellent job of starting wars at more or less the drop of a hat, usually for reasons related to the fight for resources, and for me, the old argument that religion is the root of all evil is a tired and lazy one for this reason.

True, meaningful belief systems – of which religions form the vast majority on this planet, particularly the monotheistic faiths of Christianity, Judaism, and Islam – should result in respect, compassion, and fair treatment for all, including those who don't believe. To deny completely the value of belief systems that the majority of people on the face of this earth subscribe to is both counterintuitive and an example of throwing the baby out with the bath water.

Speaking of water, imagine a group of people afloat in a boat on the ocean. The boat is a structure which both constrains us and keeps us safe, ensuring our survival. Not everyone necessarily appreciates the boat to the same degree. Some may take issue with the way it has been built and operates. They might prefer a different approach. They might decide to start taking the boat apart, either because they want a different boat, or perhaps because they don't believe they need it at all and will be just fine without it. Maybe they even make a point of setting fire to it, so they can keep themselves warm for a while. There is an epic fail here – the failure to appreciate that the very boat they don't like, think they can do without, and maybe even intend to destroy is the one thing that keeps them alive and gives them the luxury of contemplating all of this in safety, instead of fighting for their lives alone on the ocean.

Those who want to take apart the boat, or (to use a different analogy) kick away the foundations of the society that we have built, need to have a vision for what is going to replace it. As well as having a vision for how this will work, they need to have a way of sharing that vision with all the other people on the face of the earth, so that they can buy into it, share these values, and agree to live their lives accordingly. There's a word to describe people who have a shared vision and live by a shared set of values . . . Wait, it's on the tip of my tongue. No, it's gone. It will come back to me.

Effects of loneliness

I've defined loneliness and outlined some of the reasons why I believe it's an increasing challenge for us, individually and as a society. So what, I hear you ask? If being lonely simply means being sad, then what's the big deal? Loneliness is a natural part of the human condition, as I've already said. Transient loneliness is normal and necessary. Chronic (by which I mean long-term) loneliness however is a very different issue. Like sleep deprivation, being sedentary, and eating too much of the wrong kind of food, loneliness is toxic.

In terms of where it belongs on the scale of toxicity, loneliness may be worse for our health than obesity or physical inactivity, and as bad as smoking. In a review of over thirty years of global trial data (from 1980 to 2014), a strong association was found between social isolation and premature death, with the risk increasing by a shocking 30 per cent, knocking years off life expectancy.[2] Premature death was from all causes, rather than any particular disease, and was no respecter of gender or ethnicity.

Two issues identified in this meta-analysis concern me particularly, apart from the significantly increased relative risk of early death: one was that it didn't make any difference whether the social isolation was subjective or objective (i.e. whether people felt isolated or were classified as isolated, the end result was the same); and the other was that social isolation was more likely to predict death in those under 65 years of age, rather than the very frail elderly as you might have expected. Could this indicate that we have a ticking time bomb for our younger, loneliest generation in years to come?

To flip things around we also need to look at the benefits of relationships when it comes to happiness. The Study of Adult Development, conducted by Harvard University, is the longest study of happiness.[3] It has been going for 75 years and is now on its fourth director, Dr Robert Waldinger. In that time, it has followed the lives of 724 men, of whom approximately 70 are still alive. They are divided into two groups: one group is composed of Harvard graduates; the other of local men from Boston, most of whom came from much more deprived backgrounds. The data collected includes interviews and medical records. Dr Waldinger did a TED talk on the findings which is worth watching.[4] To summarize, there have been three lessons that have been learnt from the study so far:

- People with good relationships are happier and healthier, and live longer. Those that invested in new relationships after retirement (turning 'workmates' into 'playmates') did the best.

- The quality of close relationships is key and provides long-term benefit. Living in conflict is bad for us. Those who were most satisfied with relationships aged 50 were the healthiest at 80.

- Good relationships may also protect brain function.

As is said time and time again in the world of evidence-based medicine, association is not causation. If we accept that there is a strong association between loneliness and worse health outcomes, even premature death, the next question should be whether the former causes the latter, and if so, then how? If you've already read some of the previous chapters in this book, particularly the one on having a renewed mind (Chapter 8), you will probably have guessed what's coming next. If so, well done — you are clearly getting the hang of this.

It's all about inflammation. When we are hungry, we eat. When we are thirsty, we drink. When we are lonely, we reach out to people. Being close to people makes us feel safe. If we can't achieve this, if we can't feel safe, then we end up in a state of high alert, with the inevitable activation of the sympathetic nervous system and being in a state of fight or flight, with the resulting chemical cascade. This, as we now know, ultimately results in us being in an inflamed state, with all the associated risks of chronic disease, both physical and mental, that we have already discussed. Whether we are sleep-deprived, sedentary, eating ultra-processed food, stressed-out, or lonely, it's the same mechanism; the same final common pathway and the same end result.

Loneliness doesn't just mean a shorter life; it means a more painful one. The pain of loneliness is not just emotional. Social isolation activates some of the same centres in the brain that are activated by physical pain.[5] Being lonely literally hurts. A person can get into a vicious circle of developing pain, which affects their wellbeing as a result, which in turn can cause more pain. Some people are genetically predetermined to be more sensitive to pain than others, in the same way that people have different sensitivities to opiates. But it's not just our genes that determine how much pain we feel. Social support can reduce activity in the pain areas of the brain.[5]

When someone is isolated – for example, when bullied and excluded at school – they feel real pain. Think about how we self-medicate when in physical pain. People take the same approach with the pain caused by loneliness, hence the problems with drug addiction that are so often seen. Dr Gabor Maté, a world expert on addiction and author of *In the Realm of Hungry Ghosts*, says that when we are talking to someone suffering from addiction, we should ask them not why they behave as they do, but rather what the source of their pain is.[6]

Over the years I have referred many patients to pain clinics. These are the places of last resort for people suffering from long-term, pain-related problems, for which no further medical or surgical intervention is planned or possible. At the risk of doing down my colleagues who specialize in these areas, my experience is that the approach is largely one size fits all and rarely effective. It consists of either carrying out procedures or prescribing various drugs, whether opiates or other sorts of drugs that affect the nervous system. It doesn't really matter which drug is chosen as, in my admittedly jaundiced experience after twenty years of making such referrals, it rarely makes any meaningful difference, but they are pretty much all guaranteed to cause unpleasant side effects, including drug addiction.

Nowadays there is recognition that some psychological input might be appropriate; an acceptance driven by the increasing realization that the drugs don't work, they just make you worse. However, this input is offered primarily with the end goal that a person accepts and lives with their pain. This may be appropriate for some conditions, for example, by degenerative back conditions causing neurological problems, or the consequences of scarring after surgery. However, many patients are referred to the clinic because all investigations have been negative and no cause for their pain has been found. In my experience, many such patients also have histories of mental health problems and emotional trauma. However, not once have I read a clinic letter which recommends social support and a focus on building up their connections with others. They are effectively being treated as palliative.

Would we tell someone with pain from blocked coronary arteries, a broken bone requiring surgery, or a cancer that needed removing, that the best thing they can do is just put up with the pain and maybe take some drugs? Of course not. But for many people suffering from emotional and physical pain caused by loneliness and isolation, that is what we are doing – telling them their condition is terminal and prescribing drugs to ease their passing, over whatever time they have left.

Loneliness in the time of coronavirus

If we weren't already convinced about the impact of loneliness on our wellbeing, as I write this the entire world is in the middle of conducting the largest study ever into the effects of social isolation. Unlike normal medical research, there was no time spent working up protocols, considering sample size and statistical power, or seeking medical ethics approval. Instead, thanks to the coronavirus pandemic, in the spring of 2020 the world went into lockdown, an unwitting experiment that is now demonstrating the effects of social isolation on a global scale. I'm not going to discuss the disease-related havoc wreaked upon the countries and economic systems of the world by an organism so small that you need a microscope to see it, but I am interested in the unintended consequences of the loneliness pandemic, caused by our attempts to manage a viral one.

In the ongoing Covid-19 Social study, funded by the Nuffield Foundation, Wellcome, and UK Research and Innovation, lockdown has worsened overall wellbeing for at least 20 per cent of those taking part.[7] Not being able to see their friends has had the most negative impact, followed by being physically inactive and suffering from disturbed sleep. More relationships have broken down as a result, particularly in younger people. Although there has been something of a resurgence in community spirit, those that are most likely to suffer the effects of lockdown are younger people, living alone, on low incomes, with pre-existing mental health problems.

Data from the Office for National Statistics (ONS) confirms this, reporting that older adults, although more worried about the risks to their health posed by Covid-19 and pessimistic about timescale for recovery, are actually better at coping with lockdown, in terms of staying in touch with others and doing things like reading and gardening to cope.[8] Younger people are worried less about the impact of Covid on their personal health and more about its impact on their relationships, reporting higher levels of boredom and loneliness, which result in fewer of them following social-distancing guidelines, reflected in the stories reported on the front pages of the papers about such people flouting social distancing and attending illegal raves.

I'm seeing the consequences of lockdown in the lives of the patients that I consult with. In my surgery we have all noticed an emerging pattern of people presenting to us, which can be crudely divided into three categories.

In the first category, people who have historically considered themselves well and rarely consulted their doctor are now presenting with symptoms of mild depression, low mood and anxiety. Some realize this straightaway. Others take a bit of convincing that the symptoms they are describing (most commonly irritable bowel symptoms, chest pains, palpitations, and general lethargy) are actually manifestations of how they feel emotionally and mentally.

In the second category, people who have pre-existing mental-health problems (such as mild depression or anxiety) are presenting with significantly worsening symptoms, which are more likely to result in contact with mental health professionals and prescribed medication.

The third category comprises people who were already suffering from quite severe mental illness. Broadly speaking (and accepting that there will be exceptions), their symptoms don't seem to have worsened as much. I was talking to one such patient, a person in their mid-fifties with severe chronic anxiety, and asked them why they thought this was. They told me that they have effectively been living in self-imposed lockdown for years and now that everyone else was having to do the same, it actually made them feel less of an outlier and reminded them of the epitaph of comedian Spike Milligan, 'I told you I was ill.'

In medicine we use the term 'acute-on-chronic exacerbation', which is jargon for an urgent health problem caused by a flare-up of the underlying condition, such as asthma or other types of chronic lung disease. What we are seeing in the time of Covid-19 and lockdown is an acute-on-chronic exacerbation of loneliness. It has both exposed and widened the cracks in our society that already existed, hence the problems I have just described with worsening health. There may be additional longer-term consequences that we can't yet predict. Consider, for example, what effect there will be on a generation of young children raised during a time in their lives when they are denied, or discouraged from having, physical contact with others, compounded by the requirement to wear face masks in some situations. Consider the economy: how will our recovery be affected by absenteeism and reduced productivity as a consequence of loneliness?

Some of the themes I keep returning to in each chapter of this book are how we have evolved over hundreds of thousands of years, and how rapid the counterintuitive, damaging, and unnatural changes are that humankind has inflicted on itself over the last century, and even more so over the last few decades. We have sown the wind, but however bad some of us may think things are right now, we have yet to reap the whirlwind that's coming. In the relatively recent past, we experienced a global economic recession. Now in this pandemic era we are faced not just with a further economic recession, but also a social one. Will we take the opportunity instead to use what we have learnt to reverse-engineer a social revival? Have we still got time to change it?

How we can all be less lonely

Ask the question and acknowledge the problem.

The other day I was talking to a GP colleague of mine about how we carry out reviews of people with long-term conditions, such as diabetes and heart disease. It is known that people with these problems are more at risk of depression, reflected in the fact that GPs used to get paid for asking all such patients annually whether they felt depressed and offering support. I suggested to my colleague that some of the questions asked during the review should be about their personal circumstances. They looked horrified at the prospect, saying that they didn't have time to ask about that sort of thing and that they were worried it would open up a can of worms, revealing unmet needs that they were not in a position to do anything about.

I had some sympathy with this somewhat knee-jerk response, because I've been there (and in all honesty on a busy day in the practice I still end up there sometimes), but if you think about it, there's no logic to it at all. What we're saying is that we aren't interested in what would really make a difference to their quality of life, which would improve their blood pressure and blood-sugar levels as a result, but we *are* interested in making sure that they are taking tablets every day, some of which will make absolutely no difference whatsoever to their lifespan or healthspan. We are happy to offer something quick which makes very little if any difference, but not to be involved in considering longer-term solutions with multiple benefits for all concerned.

I'm not saying that a doctor can or should try to sort out someone's housing situation or relationship difficulties in their brief consultation, but we could at least recognize the problem and point them in the right direction. In doing so we might reduce that increased risk of premature death, the number of tablets they are taking (with the associated prescribing costs for the NHS), and even the number of visits to the doctor, which would of course make my colleague happy and maybe even overcome their reservations.

We should acknowledge that life is not a level playing field and we are all starting from different positions, some innately more disadvantaged than others. Just as society is important to people, so are people to society. If life is a race, then some vulnerable groups are not only disadvantaged, but not even allowed to take part. For example, people with disabilities can be viewed as limited and reaching their capacity very early on in life. We can be frightened of those who are different, who challenge our view of the world. We can be frightened by the thought of not coping with some of the challenges that they face, and of how this makes us feel when we are around them. To be mindful of such vulnerability and to protect those at risk of loneliness is not just basic decency and what they deserve, but it also brings much to our lives. My son Luke's severe epilepsy presented a real challenge to his state primary and secondary schools, which (with a bit of hand-holding and the occasional frank conversation) they rose to. We challenged those who had very low expectations for Luke. There were times we had to challenge ourselves too. As a result, it brought out the best in Luke, and in his peers and teachers, as well as providing a legacy for those that would come after him, who were also different.

Whether it's a doctor consulting with a patient, someone chatting with their neighbour over the fence, a conversation between family members, or a politician considering how best to promote fairness and wellbeing in wider society, we need to be mindful of the problem and consider how we can do our bit to help. Asking the question, whether in a one-to-one situation or via a survey for large-scale research, is important. The only reason for not asking a question is that you don't want to deal with the answer.

Offer the right solution

Even if it can be argued that, as a society, we are no more lonely than we ever were, and even if you don't believe that there are early warning signs we need to take notice of, what has definitely changed is our awareness of the impact of loneliness. Whether it's increasing or not, the consequences are no longer in doubt. So even if as a society we choose to change nothing about our default, toxic, loneliness-inducing environment, we can at least try to offer the right treatment for the problem. In the NHS, which sadly is more of a national *disease* service than a national *health* service, we have traditionally medicalized the problem of loneliness. As health professionals (and I have to include myself in this at times), either we don't diagnose the problem correctly or, much worse, we know exactly what the problem is, but we don't have the time or inclination to help people address it and resort to ineffective or palliative treatments, because this fits with our medical model, and at least it's something that we can do quickly. So, the patient leaves the consulting room clutching a sick note and a prescription for painkillers and antidepressants.

At this moment, if you are a health professional reading this you might be feeling a bit got-at and underappreciated. You might be thinking that I, as both the author of this book and a GP, should know exactly what sort of pressures you are operating under day to day and I should show a bit of empathy. By now you may suspect that I am one of those GPs who has a rug on the floor, a throw over my chair, sandals as my choice of footwear, and a waiting room full of grim-faced patients as I run over an hour behind every surgery, because of my cuddly, holistic consulting style. You would be both right and wrong. I am a GP and I do know that sort of pressures the NHS is under, particularly in primary care. However, my consulting style is best described by patients and colleagues alike as 'no nonsense': I almost never run late and my footwear of choice is a pair of black Doc Martens. I prefer plain speaking, being honest with patients about the real root cause of their problems, and both challenging and enabling them to address these in a real, meaningful way. Spending a few extra minutes in a consultation pays dividends for both the patient and the doctor, including meeting less often in future – a win for all concerned.

As professionals working in health, social care, and allied fields, we are all tools. Yes, you read that correctly. Stay with me on this one. Remember my complaint about modern medicine being a complicated tool? It's all about using the right one for the job. If you were working for the Citizens Advice Bureau advising someone on debt and noticed that they were suicidal and needed a mental health assessment, you would signpost them to a counsellor, psychologist, or doctor, rather than attempting to treat them yourself. It would clearly be inappropriate to do a quick online course in psychology or medicine, download the relevant diploma, and send them off with a prescription for drugs to manipulate their nervous system.

A doctor working in the NHS is a medical specialist, whose training has taken the best part of ten years and cost the taxpayer hundreds of thousands of pounds. Yet, when confronted with someone whose real problem is loneliness, as well as associated issues such as mental health problems or financial difficulties, instead of signposting them to someone with the right tools, they may end up attempting to do the job with the disease-based tools that they have, which were not designed for this problem. As a result, the patient not only doesn't get the help they need, but in the worst-case scenario, ends up being misdiagnosed and harmed by the wrong treatment. Sticking with the tools analogy, let's think about what we should have in our toolbox when it comes to connections.

1. Psychological techniques

These include cognitive behavioural therapy, mindfulness, and positive psychology. They have all been shown to help, and there is often a degree of overlap in these areas. Between them they cover awareness of thoughts and beliefs, challenging or rejecting them where appropriate, and developing a more positive mindset. This encourages behaviour change, including better interactions with others, which in turn then further reduces loneliness.

2. Social prescribing

These services help people to understand what matters to them and to address their needs, taking into account this whole-person view of themselves. This usually involves a health professional, such as a GP, nurse, or pharmacist, referring someone into the service where they will be allocated a link worker, who is either able to advise them directly, or to signpost them onto the relevant community service or voluntary-sector organization.

Services offered could include debt management, legal advice, cooking lessons, arts groups, gardening, physical activities, and befriending. The UK Government is sufficiently convinced of the growing evidence that this works to have invested in providing at least one social-prescribing link worker for every primary care network (group of GP practices) in the country.

As well as good feedback from service users about their improved wellbeing, it has also been shown to reduce attendances in GP surgeries and emergency departments. This has been demonstrated in Hertfordshire by such specialist practitioners, called 'community navigators'. I often suggest such an approach to my patients when I feel that the underlying reason for their consultation with me is not primarily *health*-related, but something to do with the other 80 per cent of their life that determines their sense of wellbeing.

As an aside, there is a sometimes rancorous debate (usually on social media) between those (like me), who are quite happy with the term 'social prescribing', as it bridges the medical and social parts of a person's life, and those who are deeply offended by such a term, which they consider to be too medicalized and want called something else like 'community referral'. The reality is that it's now a widely accepted term which most people can get their heads around. For me, debating exactly what we call it is either a luxury, afforded to us when we have everything so sorted that there is literally nothing else to do, or a waste of time, when we could be getting on with doing our jobs and making a difference.

3. *Valuing organizations that promote social cohesion*

This is really a bolt-on of the social-prescribing tool. It's important that the social prescribers have services in the community that they can refer people on to. There are of course lots of these, including faith-based and non-faith-based ones. It is vitally important that we do include the Church and other faith groups, as long as they are inclusive and not divisive. Shared values and codes of conduct can be really helpful. It saddens me that the Church is considered by some to be an exclusive club, when actually it should be the only one that exists for the benefit of non-members.

We need to strike the right balance between the drive to belong, which may require some conformity – for which both religious and secular society might be criticized – and the drive to develop ourselves, which requires us to stand alone and even to defy convention. I believe that our society has lurched from one extreme to the other and a course-correction is needed, to get back to the middle ground. That means some faith groups need to modernize, to become more inclusive and relinquish power and control. It also means individuals must step back into the fold from the Wild West of every person for themselves; must be honest enough to admit when they are lonely and that things aren't working out, despite their unconvincing public protestations to the contrary.

The value of the services and support provided by the Church of England (never mind all the other denominations of Christian faith) has recently been calculated at £12.4 billion a year.[9] The majority of food banks have been set up by churches. Other services provided include drug and alcohol support groups, mental health services, youth clubs, after-school care, debt counselling, and credit unions. Before anyone gets concerned about faith groups being part of the solution because of their peculiar and specific beliefs, let's remember that there are many cults in the secular world; we just don't recognize or disparage them, because they aren't religious. Instead, we give them names like 'workplace culture'. Like I said before, we all have a way of doing life, whether we realize it or not.

4. Engineering our own blue zones

I've already described the blue zones of the world, where people enjoy unusually long lifespans and healthspans. I don't know about you, but when I imagine life in a blue zone, I picture cloudless skies, white walls, terracotta roofs, people strolling around barefoot, kids playing in nature; and not a second spent worrying about the weather, Wi-Fi, email inboxes, social media, or the train timetable. I am cynical when politicians talk about importing models from other parts of the world when it comes to education or the working week, because they are the end result of the culture of a whole country, and not just a plug-in module that applies regardless of the setting.

However, we should consider the principles that we can take from the learning about the blue zones. Let's look specifically at connection, which three of these nine principles are related to. Interestingly, this makes connection the joint largest segment of the nine principles of the blue zones, along with eating wisely. These three are:

- *Belong*: Be a part of a faith-based community, regardless of denomination.

- *Loved ones first*: Keep relatives nearby. Commit to a life partner. Invest time in your children.

- *Right tribe*: Choose a small social circle that supports you for life.

Although we all face different challenges in life, I would argue that we can put some of these principles into action as best we can, whether we live in Barbagia or Blackpool.

And finally . . . address the root causes of loneliness

We've covered acknowledging the problem, asking questions, and offering the right solutions. But I've got this back to front really, because all of those are reactive. How can we be proactive? Could we aspire as a society to vastly reducing or even eliminating loneliness? I've shared my theories with you as to why we are lonely as a society. It's big-picture stuff. It's fine to do our best to address it bottom-up and I have already mentioned some things that we can all try, and there are more suggestions in my prescription for connecting at the end of this chapter. However, we do also need a top-down approach, and for most of us this is beyond our control.

Just as we need a national approach to eating well and moving more, creating the large-scale shift we need in our environment to start to shift it from a toxic one to salutogenic (one that is good for our wellbeing), so we need the same approach to building connections and reducing loneliness. Yes, people do need encouraging to do what they can to dig themselves out of the hole of loneliness. Sometimes they also need others to reach in to help. Ultimately, we need to mend the hole that people keep falling into, rather than providing a hole-side service that patches them up afterwards, directs them to the nearest emergency department, and tells them to look where they are going next time.

It's a huge undertaking with a lot of holes to fill, including fairness, friendships, family, and faith. Some of us will be able to fill in little holes that affect us and those around us – our neighbours, our community. Some of us may be able fill in the bigger holes because of our position and influence. A select few may be in charge of deciding how the biggest holes of all in society are filled. Let us not forget that even if we are not in a position to be a filler of big holes, we get to elect those who are – and then to hold them accountable.

What can we learn about connections from the Bible?

God wants to be in a relationship with us

> Fear not, for I am with you; be not dismayed, for I am your God; I will strengthen you, I will help you, I will uphold you with my righteous right hand. (Isaiah 41: 10, ESV)

> I am the vine; you are the branches. Whoever abides in me and I in him, he it is that bears much fruit, for apart from me you can do nothing. (John 15: 5, ESV)

For our lives to be truly fulfilled spiritually, physically, emotionally, or professionally, we need to be in a relationship with God.

God cares for the lonely and so should we

> Father of the fatherless and protector of widows is God in his holy habitation. God settles the solitary in a home; he leads out the prisoners to prosperity, but the rebellious dwell in a parched land. (Psalm 68: 5f, ESV)

> For I was hungry and you gave me food, I was thirsty and you gave me drink, I was a stranger and you welcomed me. (Matthew 25: 35, ESV)

Jesus spent time with those that were considered undesirable by society, whether because of disease, disability, profession, or circumstances. He invested in relationships with them and their lives were changed as a result. It wasn't just one-way either. There were times when he sought solitude, but also many others where he enjoyed the company of others. In the parable of the Good Samaritan, used by Jesus to answer the question 'Who is my neighbour?' the Samaritan had nothing at all in common with the man that he took pity on and helped. Jesus preached mercy and kindness above theology.

Our relationships with each other are also important

Two are better than one, because they have a good return for their labour: If either of them falls down, one can help the other up. But pity anyone who falls and has no one to help them up . . . though one may be overpowered, two can defend themselves. A cord of three strands is not quickly broken. (Ecclesiastes 4: 9–12, NIV)

Walk with the wise and become wise, for a companion of fools suffers harm. (Proverbs 13: 20, NIV)

Carry each other's burdens, and in this way you will fulfil the law of Christ. (Galations 6: 2, NIV)

We are made for companionship, rather than it just being an optional extra. The practical, physical value of friendship is emphasized as well as the spiritual. We should consider carefully who we decide to surround ourselves with. Some relationships need planting, some pruning, and some weeding. Friendships are for support and challenge, in good times and bad. True friends are able to be both gentle and nurturing some of the time, and to provide challenge and tough love at others. Friendship is not a one-way street and if our relationship with someone is meaningful it will involve give and take at different times.

Believers work best as a community

And they devoted themselves to the apostles' teaching and the fellowship, to the breaking of bread and the prayers. And awe came upon every soul, and many wonders and signs were being done through the apostles. And all who believed were together and had all things in common. And they were selling their possessions and belongings and distributing the proceeds to all, as any had need. And day by day, attending the temple together and breaking bread in their homes, they received their food with glad and generous hearts, praising God and having favour with all the people. And the Lord added to their number day by day those who were being saved. (Acts 2: 42–47, ESV)

That there may be no division in the body, but that the members may have the same care for one another. If one member suffers, all suffer together; if one member is honoured, all rejoice together. Now you are the body of Christ and individually members of it. (1 Corinthians 12: 25–27, ESV)

As believers we are at our most effective in a community. We are the body of Christ, his hands and feet. We show God's love to the lonely and to each other. We are witnesses, providing salt and light. We all have different roles to play and should respect this, valuing what each of us can bring to our community. We have strength in numbers and can do more together than by ourselves when reaching out to serve the wider community around us, whether it's running a foodbank, providing a debt-counselling service, or opening up our building to community groups to build connections and support those most in need.

My prescription for being connected

For individuals

1. Cultivate your relationships

This could include creating new relationships with people that you would like to get to know better, deepening some of your existing relationships; for example, spending 10–15 minutes of uninterrupted time each day with someone that you love, or choosing to end relationships that are no longer helpful. In Okinawa, one of the blue zones, people form 'moais' – groups of five friends – for life. Think about who you would like to have in this group and invest in those friendships. Reach out to those that you have lost touch with. There's nothing wrong with being intentional and deliberate about this. Don't be embarrassed about it. The quality of your life, and of your relationship with God, is affected by the quality of your relationships with others.

2. Ask for help when you need it

It can be difficult to admit when we are having a hard time. Showing vulnerability to others both deepens your relationship and also allows them to open up too.

3. Get your relationship with technology right

Technology can be such a powerful tool to connect us with others, particularly those who don't live nearby or are isolated, and to preserve relationships that might otherwise have drifted or been lost. You might be feeling a bit Zoomed-out at the end of a day of virtual meetings and having to repeatedly tell people that they are 'on mute', but there may be someone you know who would really value even a brief call. If you plan it and put in your diary, it's much more likely to happen.

On the other hand, you may need to consider replacing some of your FaceTime with face-to-face time. Our brains don't get the same buzz from a virtual relationship. Monitor your use of social media (most smartphones will now do this for you and even give you reports). Yes, you may be 'connected', but to what and to whom? It risks taking you away from the present, even the person that you are actually sitting in the room with. Don't end up like Tilly, the character in the TV comedy series *Miranda*, who interrupts conversations with people in the same room as her by holding up her hand and repeatedly saying 'Bear with, bear with' as she disengages from real life to check out what's on her phone. Social media should be a means to an end, not the actual end itself.

4. Do things for other people

It's nice, it builds relationships and, if you want to be selfish about it, service is also recognized as a powerful antidote to any loneliness that you may be experiencing yourself.

5. Be on the lookout for loneliness

Someone who is feeling lonely may not present as distant, sitting in a corner by themselves, looking a bit miserable. They may also present as irritable, angry, performing poorly at work, and experiencing relationship difficulties. Consider this if you see any of these signs in someone and ask yourself whether loneliness might be at the root of the problem. If so, think about what you can do to help. You may not have the answer, but you could at least start by asking the question.

6. Connect to your environment

Get outside and into nature if you can. It can serve as a good reminder that there's more going on in life than just what's inside your head. It gives you perspective. It can be a way of meeting people and building connections; and, of course, physical activity is good for you, as I may have mentioned once or twice.

7. Pray together

If you pray, consider praying with others. It can be a deeply bonding experience and is an easy way to share what's going on in your life with other people, and to practise asking for help when you need it. You might feel a little self-conscious at first. Do it with someone that you trust and just go for it. My best friend and I have been praying together for quite a few years now, often in a local coffee shop on a Sunday morning after a bike ride. I hadn't thought of it as an act of witness until one of the staff came up to us one morning and suggested some prayer topics for our consideration!

For organizations

1. Lead by example

If you are a leader, whether in a secular or faith-based organization, consider what kind of example you are setting. Before you advise others on how to manage their lives and relationships, consider the state of your own. How deep are your relationships with family, friends, and colleagues? Do you have someone that provides you with support and mentorship, that you can turn to when you are struggling and need to ask for help? Leadership can be a lonely experience. Being a hero is easy. Depending on others is harder, but works out better for all concerned. Which approach are you modelling to others?

2. Consider your duty of care

As in wider society, how an organization treats the most vulnerable is a measure of its humanity. There may be people that work with you, or others that you are in a position to help. What measures are there in place to support those in your workforce who are struggling? Our GP partnership, composed of people with different backgrounds and beliefs, tends to err on the side of generosity when it comes to colleagues who are struggling with life. We recognize that the NHS can be a challenging place to work and we ask ourselves how we would like to be treated if we were facing difficulties in our lives. If you are a large- or medium-sized company, how do you fulfil your corporate social responsibility? Do you support your local community, including those affected by loneliness? Is it a tick-box exercise or a meaningful one?

3. Build a connection culture

Think about how you can encourage people to build stronger connections within your organization. This could involve setting up smaller groups or a buddy system to offer each other support, whether professionally, personally, or spiritually. In a church context, consider small groups, house groups, and prayer groups. How is each one working? Do they need growing, pruning, or weeding? We need to help people overcome the perceived stigma of talking about loneliness. Organize regular social events, and in doing so remember that one size doesn't fit all.

How can you encourage newcomers to join in and be on the lookout for anyone who is left out? Think about how you set up the environment in small groups and in your church buildings. Things to consider include how you do introductions, agreement of group rules, seating arrangements, refreshments, and other practical issues that determine how welcome people feel.

4. Accept that the times are changing and so must the Church

There's no point lamenting the diminishing of the Church's traditional power and status or the declining numbers in a pew on a Sunday morning. In fact, there's a lesson to be learnt there. If the Church is truly a club that exists for the benefit of non-members, there's no point in continuing to run it the way that the current members have always preferred it. That's doing the same thing over and over again and expecting a different result, which as we all know is considered the definition of madness.

We have been commissioned to go into the world and spread the good news, not to spend all our time amongst others who share our beliefs. Echo chambers are not a good thing and this applies equally to real-life faith communities as it does to Twitter users. Instead of spending all our time telling others how we think they should live their lives, maybe we should spend more time discussing with them how we can help them live better ones. I am not a fan of sandwich-board diplomacy. As a Christian, even I don't stop to listen to people preaching loudly and earnestly in the street. Why on earth would anyone else? The return on investment of time and energy here is somewhere between negligible and non existent. I have never changed my mind about anything substantial as a result of hearing what someone shouted through a megaphone, or because of some words I saw painted on a sign.

The power of the faith community lies in being just that – a community. The Church needs to focus on how it can serve. Befriending and supporting people, with no motive other than wanting to connect with our neighbours, those fellow humans made in God's image, results in meaningful and fruitful relationships. Spend less time debating whether there should still be an eight o'clock Sunday morning service that a handful of people come to and more time focusing on practical outreach, and how the church building can best be used to host local groups and become an essential hub, the beating heart of the community. Sartre may have been (partly) right when he declared that 'hell was other people', but if you think about it, then so is heaven.

Notes

1. Office for National Statistics, 'Measures of National Well-being Dashboard', 23 October 2019. Available at: https://www.ons.gov.uk/peoplepopulationandcommunity/wellbeing/articles/measuresofnationalwellbeingdashboard/2018-04-25.

2. J. Holt-Lunstad, T.B. Smith, M. Baker, T. Harris, and D. Stephenson, 'Loneliness and Social Isolation as Risk Factors for Mortality: A Meta-Analytic Review', *Perspectives on Psychological Science*,10: 2 (2015), 227–237.

3. Harvard Study of Adult Development. Available at: http://www.adultdevelopmentstudy.org/grantandglueckstudy.

4. Dr Robert Waldinger, 'What Makes a Good Life? Lessons from the Longest Study on Happiness', TED talk, YouTube, 25 January 2016. Available at: https://youtu.be/8KkKuTCFvzI

5. N.I. Eisenberger, 'The Neural Bases of Social Pain: Evidence for Shared Representations with Physical Pain', *Psychosomatic Medicine*, 74: 2 (2012), 126–135.

6. G. Maté, *In the Realm of Hungry Ghosts: Close Encounters with Addiction* (Toronto: Knopf Canada, 2008).

7. UCL, Covid-19 Social Study: Results. Available at: https://www.covidsocialstudy.org/results.

8. Office for National Statistics, 'Coronavirus (COVID-19) roundup: People and Social Impacts', 16 October 2020. Available at: https://www.ons.gov.uk/peoplepopulationandcommunity/healthandsocialcare/conditionsanddiseases/articles/coronaviruscovid19rounduppeopleandsocialimpacts/2020-07-03#younger.

9. National Churches Trust, 'House of Good'. Available at: https://www.houseofgood.nationalchurchestrust.org/wp-content/uploads/2020/10/House-of-Good-AW-digital-small.pdf.

10. Purpose and meaning

The purposes of a person's heart are deep waters but one who has insight draws them out. (Proverbs 20: 5, NIV)

Life, the universe and everything

What is the meaning of life? According to Douglas Adams, author of one of my favourite books, *The Hitchhiker's Guide to the Galaxy*, the answer to the ultimate question of life the universe and everything is in fact '42'. Spoiler alert – I'm not going to come up with an absolutely definite answer to this question, in what remains of this book. If I were able to, I would have asked my publisher for a much larger advance! It's a really important question, though, and one which you have probably contemplated at some point or other, even if you don't consider yourself a philosopher.

The longer you've lived, the more likely you are to have considered it. The question covers both why we are here at all, and how we ought to live. If you want to dive more deeply into the former, I recommend A *Brief History of Time* by Stephen Hawking, *The God Delusion* by Richard Dawkins, *God's Undertaker* by John Lennox, and *Darwin's Angel* by John Cornwell (written by a mix of atheist and Christian authors, in the interest of balance). I'm going to focus mainly on the latter, not because I'm running out of pages but because I believe it is inextricably linked to the other areas of wellbeing that we have considered so far.

Speaking of wellbeing, I started this book by considering how it is defined. A word often used interchangeably with it is 'happiness'. Happiness requires not only *pleasure*, which is both passing and passive, but also *purpose*, which is active and lasting. It is human nature to look for meaning and purpose in life. They aren't exactly the same thing, but since this is not a philosophy textbook, I'm going to use them more or less interchangeably for the purpose of this chapter.

Purpose: Good for the soul and the bottom line

I expected this topic would be a little harder to research, both in terms of the evidence base for living a purpose-filled life and the hazards if you don't. I was half right. The latter has proved tricky. I couldn't find any randomized, double-blind, placebo-controlled trials of purpose, or any meta-analyses of this sort of thing. It's easy to find the data that shows the harms of sleep deprivation, inactivity, obesity, and social isolation, but I didn't find any trials with titles like 'Insufficient purpose in Life as a Cause for Diabetes'. However, there is some emerging data about the beneficial effect of purpose when it comes to both individual and corporate wellbeing.

Purpose doesn't just make you feel happy, it appears to have cardiovascular benefits. Having purpose in life (PiL) appears to reduce the risk of suffering a heart attack in adults with existing coronary heart disease,[1] to reduce the risk of stroke in older adults,[2] and to protect against declining brain function.[3] These are prospective (forward-looking) studies, and assess patients at a baseline, then follow their fortunes over varying lengths of time. They are all designed to take into account the confounding variables that could influence the results, such as other health conditions and risk factors like smoking, alcohol use, and socioeconomic status. The differences in outcomes caused by having a greater sense of purpose (assessed by a standardized questionnaire and scoring system) are considered to be statistically significant, which is jargon for 'unlikely to have occurred by chance', suggesting that this is worth looking into in more depth.

In short, this is one PiL that I definitely recommend you take and it doesn't even need a doctor's prescription! We can speculate about why having a greater sense of purpose may protect against these diseases. I haven't found any trials like these regarding stress and relaxation that measured inflammatory markers and brain activation and how they responded to mindfulness, but it has been suggested that purpose, like other modifiable factors in life, may well also be anti-inflammatory.

Purpose may have benefits for companies too. Although the data is not as clear here, the case can be made that companies that have purpose and related values at their core are more likely to be successful than those whose purpose is purely profit. In their book *Built to Last: Successful Habits of Visionary Companies*, Jim Collins and Jerry Porras looked at a sample of Fortune 500 companies from 1926 to 1990, using surveys completed by their chief executive officers.[4] One of the criteria for being considered a *visionary* company included having a purpose and core ideology that was not easily changed and around which everything else was built. These visionary companies were compared to other successful companies in the same industry.

In terms of the returns to their shareholders, the visionary companies outperformed their comparators by more than six times. Clearly this is not an exact science and only shows association rather than causation, but it's certainly food for thought. Not only do great purpose-driven organizations serve their shareholders and customers well, but they also improve the lives of their employees by providing jobs and financial security, as well as working alongside other organizations. Judging by the number of team-building days I've been on where we decide what our values are (so that we can turn them into mouse mats, mugs, and wall art), I assume that this principle has become widely accepted, if not always practised as meaningfully as it should be.

If we accept that a purpose-driven life is more likely to be a satisfying and enjoyable one, this suggests that it fulfils a core need at the heart of every human being. Let's look a little more at why this might be.

Our need for meaning and purpose

In his theory of human motivation, the psychologist Abraham Maslow proposed a hierarchy of needs. You may well be familiar with them. They were famously interpreted and represented as being a pyramid; an image which most of us will probably have seen at one time or another. It has been modified over the years and there are variations to it.

The first few levels at the bottom are about how we are motivated to address deficiencies in our lives in areas such as food, rest, safety, friendships, and self-esteem. The last few levels, as we near the top of the pyramid, are more about how we are motivated by personal growth (in areas such as curiosity, knowledge, beauty, balance, meaning, achieving potential, self-fulfilment) and by the desire for transcendence, examples of which include experiences of nature, serving others (one of the five ways to mental wellbeing, of course), and the pursuit of science . . . and faith. Like all models it has its flaws. Life is also not a slow steady climb to the top of the pyramid, nor is there any guarantee of staying there, as we all move up and down levels depending on our circumstances.

It can be a little simplistic, and different people have different priorities when it comes to their own personal hierarchy of need. Even if you are hungry or poor (as many people are in different parts of the world) you can still be happy. A lot of this depends upon our values.

Where do you and I get our values from? They don't arrive fully formed with us when we are born. Are they from our parents, teachers, friends, colleagues, life experience, adverts, pithy words of wisdom on social media, or our own research? Our values will derive from some or all of those. Some of these influences are personal, and some will be the result of the messages we are given by wider society. You might be forgiven for thinking that if society, which contains a lot of wise and clever people, has the answer then it could save you a lot of trouble finding out for yourself, and we would make fewer and fewer mistakes as we progress smoothly upwards towards utopia. But you know how this works by now, don't you? I highlight an area of wellbeing and then point out how, despite it being perfectly obvious to you and me, society as a whole is going about it the wrong way, with predictably disastrous consequences. Let's take, for example, the fixation of leaders and economists the world over on the golden idol of gross domestic product (GDP).

Measuring everything except that which really matters

You may have noticed that I have stolen the above section title from a quote by Bobby Kennedy in a famous campaign speech from 1968. The subject of his criticism? Gross domestic product. GDP is defined as the total value of goods and services produced by a country in a given year. The problem with GDP is that it is just a number. It ignores a number of things such as inequality, emergency disaster spending (on things like floods and earthquakes), and the contribution made by industries that boost GDP but ultimately cost society more (e.g. pollution in manufacturing, and of course the tobacco industry). Economic growth should be one of the strands to delivering a better life for all. It should be the means to such an end, not the end itself, and not relied upon solely to deliver this better life, because it can't.

Prosperity only gets you so far. It's not true that money can't buy you happiness; it may insulate you from some of the more basic causes of misery (like starvation and homelessness). But happiness doesn't rise inexorably with income. There is a point at which being more prosperous doesn't make us any happier. This is called 'income satiation'. What's interesting is that the satiation point is much higher in richer countries, with people in poorer countries achieving maximum happiness at much lower levels of income. This suggests that the more we have, the more we think we need to be happy. I wonder whether we see the hands of the evil twins of comparison and expectation once again at work here. In fact, there may be a point at which not only does more wealth not make us any happier, but it may decrease our happiness.[5] Despite this, most governments continue to obsess over GDP.

Ultimately the world, particularly the developed world, needs to get over this and move on. It is becoming particularly important because underlying our fixation with GDP is the inherent assumption that economic growth must always continue. The maths really doesn't stack up here. It fails the reality test. To quote the economist Kenneth Boulding: 'Anyone who believes that exponential growth can go on for ever in a finite world is either a madman or an economist'. I'll come back to this later. If this is a subject that catches your imagination, I recommend Tim Jackson's *Prosperity without Growth*.[6]

Hearteningly there is some appetite for change. There are a number of other measures either proposed or in use, although not universally adopted yet. These include the Thriving Places Index (developed in the UK), the Human Development Index (created by the United Nations), and the Happy Planet Index (HPI). Interestingly the USA ranks 1st for GDP and 108th for HPI, with Costa Rica ranking 1st for the latter. Make of that what you will. They all look at things slightly differently and all have pros and cons. The Kingdom of Bhutan has a unique system called the Gross National Happiness Index, which includes questions about prayer and meditation. I rather like the sound of this, although apparently it takes three hours or more to fill in the survey.

Now let's go back to Maslow's hierarchy and GDP. Even if you are someone who feels reassured by the nice, simple, and misleading figure of GDP – and who by fortunate coincidence lives in the developed world, where the GDP figure is likely to be higher – if you don't address the issue of true meaning and purpose in your life you can only get so far when it comes to personal development, and therefore how satisfied and happy you are with life. There is a ceiling that you cannot get above without this.

You might say that you are happy with this and that not everyone will get to the top of the pyramid or expect to remain there. True, but I think that we should at least aspire to this. As I have already mentioned, our natural state is in movement and I don't mean just physical. You've heard the saying that 'life is a journey not a destination'. It isn't stable and static and so neither is our wellbeing. People on a tightrope don't stand still. If they do, they fall off. If you settle for and expect things never to get better in life, the only movement you will ever experience will be in a downward direction. So how might we start to address this? Let's start with one word.

Ikigai

Ikigai is one of my favourite words. It's Japanese, about a thousand years old and doesn't have a direct one-word equivalent in English, but translates roughly as a reason for being, or happiness in living – basically the reason why you get up in the morning. It trips off the tongues of the great and the good of the lifestyle medicine world. Why? Because it's a simple concept that everyone can understand, reflect on, and use to make life more meaningful for themselves and others. If you google the term and search for images, you will very likely see four intersecting circles used to illustrate the point that by focussing on what you love, what the world needs, what you can be paid for and what you are good at, you are more likely to be fulfilled and have purpose or "ikigai" in your life. This model is highly westernized, and quite career-focussed. It tends to be used by life coaches and wellbeing gurus who came across it after googling the term and watching a TED talk on the subject. It's not without merit but it doesn't really reflect the original concept as understood by the Japanese. I prefer the Ikigai Framework developed after in depth study of the concept by Nicholas Kemp in collaboration with one of Japan's leading ikigai authorities, clinical psychologist Professor Akihiro Hasegawa. I find it helpful as a visual guide to understanding and finding ikigai in the broadest, most holistic sense of the word.

It isn't just about income. For some it won't involve income at all. It isn't just about whether we feel happy right now, but what we aspire to in the future. The blue zones of the world have this principle in common. They might not have the same word for it, or even any word at all, but it's there. It's strongly tied in with the sense of community that I have

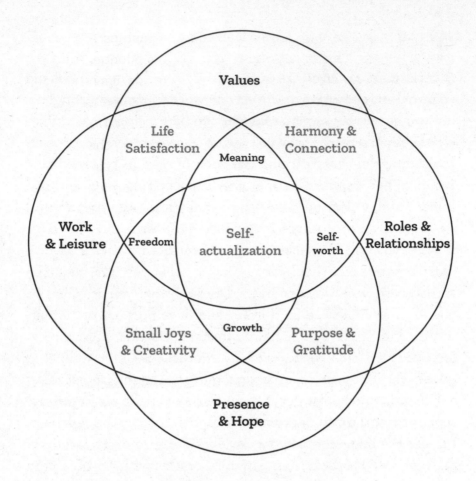

Japanese understanding of Ikigai

already mentioned. People have a stronger sense of purpose because life is not just about looking inward and serving themselves, but also about looking outward and serving their communities. As a result, the elderly are valued and remain active, contributing significantly to the lives of those around them, passing on wisdom, and teaching.

In my experience, meaning requires relationships and goals, love and work. This is another reason why I no longer think or talk about work–life balance. It's just *life* balance. It's important to be able to switch off at the end of the day, to close the laptop, and put away the phone. However, if you divide your existence mentally into 'work' and 'life', you risk developing the mindset that work is a necessary evil to be put up with and that real life can only be lived outside it. In doing so you may make it much harder to find your reason for being – your ikigai.

I used to think like this. The problem with this mindset was that I was telling myself that I was spending the vast majority of my time doing something I didn't enjoy or see the point of, even as a doctor. What a terrible waste of time! I had lost the mindset of my six-year-old self, who felt instinctively that being a doctor would be important and make a difference.

To feel differently about work I had to view it differently and do it differently. I had become disillusioned practising a disease-based, reactive model of medicine, which didn't work for most people and which I no longer believed in. It had been drilled into me in over a decade of training. It was what was expected of me and I had never thought to question it, until life intervened with a double whammy of both growing dissatisfaction that I was not able to help people with what was really wrong with them, and with the epiphany of my personal experiences at home. I'm still very much a work in progress, both personally and professionally (there are people who will happily provide signed statements to this effect!), but I am now rediscovering some of the enjoyment that I got when I started practising medicine almost a quarter of a century ago.

I'm also discovering new things as I do my job in a different way. It's not without its challenges. It can take more time to do it properly. It can mean difficult conversations with patients, who have also only ever experienced this disease-based approach and feel uncomfortable with the idea that they need to take a lot more personal responsibility to prevent and manage health problems, and not rely upon a doctor trying (and failing) to fix it for them. Not all of my colleagues share my views about how we should work, or even if they do agree with me, they are not yet in a place where they feel able to do this for themselves.

Going back to my favourite recurrent theme about environment, I believe that rather than blaming individual health professionals for not yet being ready to change the habits of a lifetime, what is required is a new default setting, with the right system in place to enable change individually and collectively. There's growing momentum behind the lifestyle-medicine movement and the future is potentially exciting. There have been models of the consultation in general practice that we have been using and tweaking for decades. I believe that there are some bits worth keeping, and a lot that needs throwing out. It's time for a wellness-based model, but that's a topic for another book.

You may be thinking that it's easy for me to talk about work and purpose because I'm a doctor, with some of this stuff built into my job. There's some truth in this. Fewer and fewer people now have conventional careers for which they train and then spend the rest of their lives doing. As we live longer, we may well have a number of different roles in our lives, whether at work, in our family, or within our communities. You may not consider your job to be important, glamorous, well-paid, or fulfilling. Not everyone is going to be rich and famous, or win accolades. We can't be, despite the messages that we are sometimes given as we grind our way up the greasy pole of the education system and look at other people's stories on social media. Social mobility, like stocks and shares, may go down as well as up. We won't all be better educated, wealthier, and more fulfilled than our parents, and the same goes for our kids and their kids.

However, I believe that people can find nobility in what they do. Not in the dystopian way that is presented in Aldous Huxley's *Brave New World*, where society is engineered and citizens are assigned roles in an intellectual hierarchy, but in a real, pragmatic way. We can all serve and leave the world a better place than we found it, in however small a way. You may be familiar with the story of the janitor working at NASA who, when asked by President John F. Kennedy what he did there, responded by saying that he was helping to put a man on the moon. My son has a moderate learning disability and severe epilepsy. He thrives on having a sense of purpose. He volunteers in a food bank and sings in a community choir. All his life he has inspired those around him because of his positive and uncomplaining nature and can-do attitude.

If we all had the meaning of life sussed in the first couple of decades of our lives, the world would be a very different place. It's a journey. You don't always need to know exactly where you are going when you set out. Some of it can be figured out along the way and your experience of travelling may well shape your plans and your final destination. Because of this evolving process very few of us will be able to say that we have reached 'the end' of a long-distance, meticulously planned journey during our lifetime. Don't be disheartened by this. In fact, I would argue that you should not expect or even aim for this because achieving it may suggest your life goals were very modest indeed. Think of it as a series of waypoints. When you've reached one, it may become clearer what the next one is. Don't spend all your time worrying about reaching the end of the line. Take time to enjoy the ride.

Just as I've argued that the physical, mental, and spiritual shouldn't be considered separate, nor should the different pillars of wellbeing. Considering the meaning of your life, what your purpose may be, and how it may change over time is not something to be done in a vacuum. If we are to move on from *imagining* our purpose to *fulfilling* it, we need to be living a lifestyle that enables this: sleeping well, moving more, eating good food, and living mindfully. Improving these areas will help you with understanding your purpose. Having a purpose will help you to live better. To use a physics analogy, just like lightbulbs in an electrical circuit they should be wired in parallel, rather than in series. That way, you don't need to have achieved perfection in one area before being able to move on to the others, and the energy that you need to achieve purpose will be available to you.

I hope that by now I have made the case for the importance of purpose in your life if you are to enjoy true wellbeing and fulfilment. I've done this in fairly broad, agnostic terms without focusing on specific belief systems. As a Christian I accept completely that you can live a fulfilling and purposeful life, whichever philosophy or faith you practise, whether you can articulate it or not. I believe that we are all made in God's image, whether we believe it or not, and that we share common characteristics as a result. I don't believe that people who are religious are better than those who are not. I do believe, however, that faith reaches the parts that other philosophies cannot, when it comes to meaning and purpose in your life. I believe that the denigration of faith is harmful and that we ignore this at our peril, individually and collectively. Gus Speth, an American professor of law and environmental advisor to two US presidents, once said:

> I used to think the top environmental problems were biodiversity loss, ecosystem collapse and climate change. I thought that with thirty years of good science we could address these problems. But I was wrong. The top environmental problems are selfishness, greed and apathy, and to deal with those we need a spiritual and cultural transformation, and we scientists don't know how to do that.

Evidence for faith and meaning as part of wellbeing

Faith is a normal and healthy aspect of human nature. Its rituals mark life's milestones and mysteries. I have no problem with those who don't share my faith, who have a different operating framework. However, those who demand loudly that it be banished from the public sphere, or even go further in saying that it shouldn't even be practised privately, demonstrate profound ignorance of the human condition into which faith can give such insight.

Faith is described in the dictionary as having trust and confidence in something or someone. I like the Message version of the Bible verse in Hebrews 11: 1, which says, 'The fundamental fact of existence is that this trust in God, this faith, is the firm foundation under everything that makes life worth living. It's our handle on what we can't see'.

I'm not using this platform to debate the existence of God, or to compare one religion against another. That's a different book and not one that I am ever likely to write. I'm of the opinion that debating God into existence is neither possible nor required of us. However, I am going to present the evidence for the wellbeing-related benefits of having faith, which is somewhat easier and is consistent with the approach I have taken with the other pillars of wellbeing discussed so far.

In 2016, Theos, a think tank interested in an understanding of faith as a force for good in society, published a report called *Religion and Wellbeing: Assessing the Evidence.*[7] It looked at 139 studies in over 30 years of data. Let's start with a disclaimer: the report acknowledged that correlation is not causation (by which I mean that just because two things appear to be linked doesn't prove definitively that one causes the other). This is, of course, true of all data in any study or report, and it doesn't stop us discussing what the data might mean and what the next steps could be in any other sphere of life. Nor should it stop us with regard to faith. Key findings from the report were:

- The more serious, genuinely held, and practised a religious commitment is, the greater the effect on wellbeing.

- Having a religious belief can give your suffering meaning, and provide a framework for coping with whatever life throws at you.

- Belief alone, without a personal practice or participation, does not promote wellbeing, and may even reduce it.

Mere religious affiliation and religiosity (identifying yourself as follower of a particular religion and having outward displays of piety) has the weakest correlation with wellbeing. Personal religious belief has a positive effect on wellbeing, made stronger when participating with others. This makes perfect sense. Merely deciding what group you identify with and what label you wear doesn't necessarily mean that this shapes your mindset and how you live day to day. After all, anyone can join a gym and pay their membership fees. The ones likely to stick at it and benefit most are those that attend regularly and participate with others.

In other words, just like other aspects of lifestyle medicine, such as sleep, exercise, nutrition, and connection, you need the right dose. It would be interesting to see if there is a dose-response curve when it comes to religiosity and spirituality. Does doing a little, like the person who takes those first steps off the couch to start moving, give the greatest relative gains in wellbeing? Should faith, like everything else, be practised in moderation? Is there a sweet spot on the curve for each one of us? If you practise your faith to extremes, does it stop making your life better, as it crowds out other important aspects of life and increases the risk of spiritual or moral injury? I'm not saying that we shouldn't aspire to deepening our faith, rather that we should consider how we interpret this in the way we then live our lives, spend our time, and interact with other people.

I've certainly seen undesirable outcomes in the church community when, not content with agreeing on the fundamentals such as the teachings of Jesus and the need to spread the good news, people instead seek out smaller and smaller points of doctrine over which they can fall out spectacularly. This is not confined to religion of course. It applies to any strongly held beliefs about how we should be doing life, such as in education, the economy, and the environment.

It's all about the stories we tell ourselves. Positive narratives flow through your life and into others. Destructive narratives lead to destructive habits. Whatever faith a person practises, doing it sincerely, driven by intrinsic motivation, rather than the extrinsic motivation of participating as a means to an end (such as getting a ticket to heaven or being approved of socially), is the key. Wellbeing should be the logical, happy side effect of a meaningful belief system, rather than the reason for taking it up.

. . .

I've described in rather general terms the evidence for faith enhancing wellbeing. So far so vague and subjective, you might say. What about the specifics? Let's start with revisiting the blue zones and longevity. The Blue Zones Project, set up by Dan Buettner, recommends a number of lifestyle habits as a result of their research. One of them is a sense of belonging. The vast majority of centenarians (258 out of 263) interviewed for the project by the *National Geographic* team belonged to faith-based communities. It was noted that there was a correlation between their longevity and attendance at regular faith-based services, regardless of denomination.

A study conducted at Harvard University and published in *JAMA Internal Medicine* found that regular attendance at religious services was associated with significantly lower risk of death from all causes, including cardiovascular disease and cancer, among women. It concluded that 'religion and spirituality may be an underappreciated resource that physicians could explore with their patients as appropriate'.[8] These are, of course, the conclusions of just one study. What about analysing multiple studies?

Well, since you asked, another study looked at systematic reviews of mortality and compared standard health interventions with religiosity and spirituality. A positive correlation was found between faith and mortality that was better than over half of the other standard health interventions, and probably the equivalent of eating the recommended daily amount of fruit and vegetables or taking a statin.[9] Maybe there's hope yet for those that want to invest in their wellbeing but don't like the idea of eating kale, or swallowing pills.

These are examples of research conducted on initially healthy populations. What about the bigger challenge of those who are already affected by disease? There's evidence here too. One such study, looking at the effect of spiritual coping, followed up people with a diagnosis of HIV over the next seventeen years. Even after allowing for differences in individual health behaviours, adherence to medication, abstinence from drug abuse, and levels of social support, it found that there was a statistically significant association between spiritual coping and increased survival.[10] People using these spiritual coping strategies (which included positive reframing, gratitude, and overcoming guilt) were 2–4 times more likely to be alive by the end of the study.

As I've said before, I'm not using any of this to argue for the existence of God or to promote a particular faith over others, even though I am a Christian. I'm just reinforcing the point that having meaning and purpose in life is important for our wellbeing (remember the top of the pyramid?), and that practising an active faith is a clear example of this. I'm not advocating faith on prescription. This would make a lot of people feel very uncomfortable and anyway, as we now know from the available evidence, it wouldn't work. It does however raise the question of how considering spirituality might play a part not just in our personal lives but in clinical care.

I have never deliberately introduced the subject of my personal faith into a doctor–patient consultation uninvited. This is a bit of a taboo in Western medicine, for largely understandable reasons. However, many of us as doctors will have shared our personal life experiences to the benefit of the patients that we consult with. It's interesting that we place this arguably artificial divide between those areas, when in fact they are all part of life and make us what we are. I have however had patients who follow various different creeds ask me to pray with them or for them, despite their not knowing where I stand on this, but I am never offended by this as a medical practitioner. As a Christian I am able to agree to their request and to support them in this authentic and meaningful way.

There is also evidence of benefit from spiritual practices outside of organized religion, such as yoga. There isn't enough clear data yet to demonstrate the superiority of organized religion vs general spirituality. This offers hope to those who aren't signed-up members of a particular spiritual club. You may not feel in a place to consider following a particular faith. This might be because it has just never been on your radar. It might be because you don't feel comfortable putting all your eggs in one basket. It may be that bad experiences have left you either never wishing to explore this, or led you to reject the faith that you once knew.

What about those who do not believe? What about those for whom the word 'spirituality' conjures up toe-curling images of people hugging trees, growing their own clothes, praying to a non existent being, or attempting yogic flying? One of my closest friends is an avowed atheist. I don't just mean he hasn't thought about the existence of God much or that he has his doubts — it's his deeply held belief. He has the same zeal for his atheism as I have for my Christian faith. He describes the Bible as my 'big book of stories'. We met on the first day of secondary school, over thirty-five years ago. We have enjoyed sparring affectionately over the decades. Putting aside the matter of whether there actually is a God, what are the implications for those like my friend when it comes to wellbeing?

Let's go back to basics. At the heart of it all is meaning and purpose. If it were possible for us all to have this, regardless of creed or philosophy, we would be better off individually and collectively. As I write these words it's an early, rainy Sunday morning in October. I'm sitting in the kitchen drinking tea, listening to my favourite writing music and pondering what words should go on the page next. At the start of writing this paragraph I text my friend to ask him to sum up what his purpose and meaning in life is. He answers straightaway: he considers his biological purpose is to pass on his genes. However, what gives his life meaning is to live by and build on the moral code that he has developed from his upbringing and experiences: to see friends grow, succeed, and persevere in the face of tragedy, and to be accountable for how he lives his life and to be part of a society that nurtures these same values. To leave the world with one less tear and one more smile because of his life and actions overall. In his view, the final destination is the same, even if he and others are not driven by a belief in a higher power.

I can't disagree with these principles. To the casual observer, how we live our lives might not look very different. The main difference between my friend and I is that I believe we are all made in God's image, whether we believe it or not. Humanity therefore shares some common core values and traits, whatever we consciously consider our personal drivers. We will definitely all do better for having purpose and meaning in our lives. We all have rules of life whether we realize it or not. To live a whole and purpose-filled life, fulfilling all our potential, requires a breaking down of the wall, a bridging of the divide between what we consider the spiritual and the secular. We limit our growth as spiritual beings if we ignore our humanity, and we cannot achieve our full potential as humans if we ignore our spirituality.

Having thrown down a bit of a challenge to people who follow no particular faith, I'd like to throw one down to followers of a particular faith — my own. There is a balance to be struck here in considering the place of faith in terms of our wellbeing. I started this book talking about the need to not separate the physical from the spiritual. It is true that faith helps us to cope with the different challenges we face in life. There is some objective evidence of this, as I have described. For me, it cuts both ways. Faith should not just be a badge or a label, mere religiosity. The fruit of our relationship with

God should be observable and measurable. If someone tells me that they have lots of spiritual gifts (such as prophecy, discernment, speaking in tongues, etc.), but their physical and mental health, their relationships, their career or finances are a disaster, I would question whether they truly understand what wellbeing really means, and whether they've got the balance right.

Let's take a look at what the Bible calls 'fruits of the spirit': love, joy, peace, patience, kindness, faithfulness, and self-control. Surely these will result in better mental health, physical health, and relationships? Please don't misunderstand me. I'm not preaching some misguided prosperity doctrine, suggesting that if you have 'true faith' you will automatically end up with a better job or a bigger house, and that everything in your life will be great. I'm also definitely not suggesting that any problems in your life, or the lives of your family or friends, are due purely to insufficient faith or some ancestral wrongdoing. There's no judgement from me if you or your loved ones are suffering with mental health problems, relationship breakdown, disease or debt – particularly if you are carrying pain from what has happened to you in life. That said, the proof is ultimately in the fruit that you bear.

Perfection, the enemy of the good, is not required (were it even possible), but progress should be evident. How else can you be effective in your own life and affect the lives of others? Just like the business leader who writes a policy on workforce wellbeing, but doesn't actually look after themselves or others, or the Christian who turns up to take part in a Sunday morning service struggling with sleep deprivation, drug or alcohol problems, weight and malnourishment issues, or relationship difficulties, we are all ultimately accountable. We don't need to be perfect to be accepted by God or useful to others. We do need to be honest about the journey that we need to take, and to actually be on the journey, rather than just preaching and singing earnestly about it.

What can we learn about meaning and purpose from the Bible?

God has a purpose for your life

> For we are God's handiwork, created in Christ Jesus to do good works, which God prepared in advance for us to do. (Ephesians 2: 10, NIV)

> And we know that in all things God works for the good of those who love him, who have been called according to his purpose. (Romans 8: 28, NIV)

> All authority in heaven and on earth has been given to me. Therefore go and make disciples of all nations, baptizing them in the name of the Father and of the Son and of the Holy Spirit, and teaching them to obey everything I have commanded you. And surely I am with you always, to the very end of the age. (Matthew 28: 18–20, NIV)

Our lives are not simply random events generated in chaos by an uncaring engine that has been set in motion and left to churn away. God is a god of meaning and purpose, and this is reflected in his creation. We are not simply automatons made to exist, pass on our genes, and then die. We are made in his image. Jesus himself gave all his disciples, including us, his great commission to go into all the world. He also reassures us that we are not alone and he is always with us. We have a hope and a future. We will all have different callings, whether in formal ministry or just being salt and light in our communities through the way that we live our lives day to day.

When I was younger and less knowledgeable than I am now, I imagined the mission field was a faraway place, where missionaries would risk life and limb hacking their way through the jungle to discover lost, primitive tribes who had never heard the Gospel. I imagined that malnourishment was a disease confined largely to the developing nations. I couldn't have foreseen that people would face malnourishment, both physically (I dislike the misleading term 'overnutrition') and spiritually in the 'developed' world in which we now live. If you don't get what your body needs from what you eat, you are physically malnourished no matter how many calories of junk-food you consume. If you don't get what your soul needs for living a purposeful, happy life, you are spiritually malnourished no matter how much time you spend tasting all the different junk-food philosophies out there that clamour loudly for your attention.

In addition, very few of us in the developed world will, thankfully, ever face physical malnourishment due to starvation. However, the risk to our wellbeing as individuals and as a society, due to the misguided denigration of faith, presents us with this unfortunate double whammy of both spiritual malnutrition and starvation.

When children have baptism or dedication services at our church there is usually a point in the service at which people are invited to share any words of knowledge that they have about the child in question, by which I mean anything they feel that God is saying about them. I am struck by how grand many of these visions are, in term of the claims made about the impact these infants are going to have on the world. That's a lot of responsibility for someone who can't even walk or talk yet. It would be interesting to follow these individuals over the course of their lives and see how many of these words and prophecies come true.

The slightly sceptical point I'm trying to make here is that however lovingly well-intentioned these bold and kind words are from friends, family, and godparents, not every child will go on to set the world alight. Most will not become famous Christian teachers or world leaders. There is however nothing wrong with this at all. In fact, it's the norm. My prayer for them is that they find purpose and meaning in their lives and that, whatever circumstances they find themselves in, they will minister to others in one way or another, however remarkable or unremarkable, whatever that means.

Prioritize spending time seeking purpose

What our exact calling is, what the specific good works are that we have been created to do, are things we need to give ourselves time to ponder and discover.

The purposes of a person's heart are deep waters, but one who has insight draws them out. (Proverbs 20: 5, NIV)

But more than anything else, put God's work first and do what he wants. Then the other things will be yours as well. (Matthew 6: 33, CEV)

Imagine getting into a car to make a journey without having given any thought to why you are making it or where you are going. Without at least an idea of your destination, maybe having consulted your satnav in the process, the chances of you getting to where you need to go and doing whatever you need to do are absolutely tiny. If you wouldn't drive your car like this, why would you live your life like it? You don't need to have every last turn planned. You might end up driving round in circles for a while, get stuck in traffic, decide to take a diversion, or even change your final destination along the way. Now I'm not suggesting that we can only live a truly meaningful life if every moment is planned and we know what every single minute will hold. Life's not like that.

For over ten years as a family our plans had to be sketchy outlines at best and for longer periods if we had any sense of purpose it was basically for our son Luke to still be alive at the end of day, and the rest of us to have our sanity more or less intact. We are actually warned in Luke 12: 20 against being like a rich man who makes grand plans for the future, unaware that his life is about to end and his plan come to nothing. In Proverbs 19: 21 we are reminded that whatever and however many plans we have in our heart, the Lord's purpose will prevail.

So what line should we tread when it comes to purpose and plans? My view is that we should all spend time dedicated to thinking about purpose in life, whether it's just having a few minutes every now and then to think about our ikigai, or spending time praying and reading the Bible. For many years I would regularly ask God to make his clear his purpose, to reveal his good, pleasing, and perfect plan for my life. There were times when it was very hard to see. There have been very few moments in my life where I have been aware of what you might call divine inspiration, with the big finger of God pointing down out of the sky and saying 'it's you!' I don't think that God works like this, for most of us.

When I was younger, I used to imagine that whatever I wanted to do in life wouldn't necessarily be what God wanted for me. My take on childhood teachings was that the Christian life was one of sacrifice and whatever God had intended for me was not necessarily going to be pleasant or easy. I was Jonah, and somewhere out there was a very big fish with my name on it. As I have lived and learnt, my relationship with God has evolved. When it comes to purpose in life, I have continued to take stock at regular intervals, and sometimes ask specific questions of God out loud. As a Christian, I don't think there's necessarily a lot of difference between those two approaches.

Your life may have many purposes

> There is a time for everything, and a season for every
> activity under the heavens. (Ecclesiastes 3: 1, NIV)

Defining ourselves as existing to serve one function, to achieve one thing, is pretty restrictive. What happens with the rest of our lives, particularly when the big thing that we consider our purpose doesn't appear to be progressing as well as we might like, if at all? Our relationships and roles are key to our sense of purpose. You may be a father, a mother, a sibling, a child, a friend, a volunteer, a colleague, a boss, a believer, or a leader. You may be at the start or the end of a particular career, thinking of changing direction, asking yourself big questions about your faith, or have particular interests outside what you think of as your day job.

One of my roles is to appraise and support other doctors. I get the privilege of spending time with them one to one every year. One part of the appraisal process is to agree on their personal development plan (PDP). This can include things like updates on particular clinical topics, developing a new skill or role, or making changes within their GP practice. I also encourage my appraisees to consider their own wellbeing, and we have included things like developing a mindfulness practice, working on their family relationships, or learning a new language. Then the following year we discuss how much of their PDP they achieved. There is usually a mixture of objectives which have been achieved, modified, postponed, or abandoned. This is absolutely fine by me because it reflects real life. It's unusual to have one item that remains on the PDP year after year. So, it is with our purpose in life. We might have a broad vision and a general direction but the specifics will change over time.

Having said that there have been very few times in my life where I could honestly say that God has spoken to me directly, one such time was on 15 April 2018, around 8.30 on a cloudy Sunday morning. I know this, thanks not to a photographic memory (cue hollow laughter from my wife), but the journalling app I keep on my phone. I was riding my mountain bike through the beautiful Gorhambury Estate in St Albans. I climbed off my mud-spattered bike, propped it up against a gate across the track I was riding on, and was taking in both a drink and the view of the trees and fields around me. In that moment I was convinced that I should write a book about wellbeing. It was to be broad, with something for everyone, putting together everything I had learnt and synthesizing it into something digestible and accessible. Faith needed to be an important part of it, so it wasn't just another book written by a doctor about wellbeing.

There was no audible voice, no earthquake or wind or fire, just complete and instant conviction. The timing made sense. I was at a place in my life where our family situation was calmer and more settled, with Luke now living away from home in a lovely setting in which he was thriving. I started writing that day. The next eighteen months were a mix of blogging, reading, attending courses, having conversations with like-minded people, listening to podcasts, making notes, and trying to develop some sort of coherent framework. My long-suffering family, particularly my wife, supported me in giving me the time that I needed to do this, mainly in early mornings before work and on Saturdays. I spent hours reading advice on writing, getting an agent, and getting published. It looked pretty daunting, but I cracked on.

I eventually submitted my non fiction proposal to any publisher or agent that might conceivably be interested, and quite a few that in all probability were not. Most agents and publishers tell

10. PURPOSE AND MEANING

you that if they haven't replied to you in three months, then it's a 'no'. I got a lot of rejection emails from the great and the good, all saying the same thing: not quite right for them; bit of a crowded market, and so on. The three months elapsed, and then elapsed some more. I was wondering whether I had got it wrong or needed to take a different approach.

Coronavirus intervened and the plans of the entire world were thrown into chaos. I put writing aside. Then one day, deep into the pandemic lockdown and in the middle of a virtual surgery, my phone rang. When the person on the end of the phone introduced themselves, I was so stunned that my first thought was that it was very nice of them to go to the trouble of ringing to reject me in person, rather than just sending me an email. When someone from a major publisher tells you that they get what you are about, that it fits perfectly with what they want, their team are excited and on board, and they'd like to publish your book, it's a pretty big moment.

Fast-forward through finding a great agent who shares my vision and signing a contract, here I sit on yet another Saturday morning tapping away and sipping tea, mindful of the submission deadline in exactly three weeks. If you're reading this, it all turned out okay.

The long-winded point I'm trying to make is that this is one of my purposes – for now. I don't know what will come of my writing this book. I don't know whether you're reading this because you found it in a bargain bin at a discount bookshop, or because you saw it advertised on a bestseller list. I'm open to what comes next. I did a deal with God when I was twelve years old. I remember the night. I told him that I would be willing to follow whatever purpose he had for my life, and all I asked was that he made it pretty clear when the time was right. I'm doing my best to stick to the deal.

The next thing could be something I have never imagined. More likely, it will be something that my life experience and training has equipped me to do. God may well move in mysterious ways, but I think he's pretty comfortable with moving in really obvious ones too.

My prescription for living life on purpose

For individuals

1. Start by asking yourself questions

Think about the following areas: your values, your roles, your purpose, and life satisfaction. When are you living your values? What do you do that makes life worth living? What gives you a sense of purpose and life satisfaction? Why? Write down two or three answers for each of these areas.

2. Plan purposefully

Once you've worked out what matters to you and are developing some ideas of your purpose/s, consider what goals you might have in relation to these. What are the steps along the way? What might get in the way? How might you plan to overcome these obstacles?

3. Take yourself on a retreat

Even if you don't have the time or the finances to spend a weekend in splendid contemplative isolation, you can take a DIY approach. Rest is vital for creativity. You could start just by building a few minutes of peace and quiet into each day (or maybe a longer session once every week or two), whether at home or at work, to ask questions and do the planning necessary for points 1 and 2 above. Think about where you could do this and when. Who do you need to tell about this, so they can support you in making it happen? It might be your spouse, housemate, or boss. If you have a faith, consider combining this time with prayer, reading, or meditation. Remember that all these aspects of your life are interconnected.

4. Remember the happiness equation

Consider your reality and your expectation. The equation needs balancing, whether this is by you being able to improve your reality or manage your expectations. 'Managing expectations' gets bad press because it's often used in a negative context; that is, don't expect too much out of life when there aren't enough resources to go around. Actually, it can be really helpful. Why not swap an unattainable life of perfection for one that is real and fulfilling?

5. Think about how you view work

Is what you get paid for a job or a calling? Can it be both? Can you turn one into the other? Viewing it differently may help how you feel about and do your job. That said, if you feel that your job is entirely incompatible with what you enjoy, what you are good at, and what the world needs, then maybe consider whether you need to make a change as circumstances allow. I recommend ditching the concept of 'work–life balance'. Your work is part of your life. If you only allow yourself to enjoy and find meaning in the parts of your day that aren't spent in paid employment, you're not going to have much opportunity for life satisfaction.

6. Purpose is more powerful when shared

Although it's good to have relationships with others that are different from you, who challenge and enrich your life when you do the same for them, there are times when you need the company of like-minded people. If you have a shared purpose, whether in a secular or faith-based group, you can support and encourage each other. Some goals will be more easily achieved together. Feeling that you are achieving your purpose or purposes in life will strengthen you and encourage you to do more.

For organizations

1. Develop your vision and values

Is your company, your GP practice, your hospital trust, church or community group a visionary one? Have you identified a shared purpose, built around those that you are meant to serve? Do you give yourselves time to do this?

2. Lead by example

If you want your organization to live and breathe your vision and values, you need to set the tone. What sort of example do you set to those for whom you are responsible? How easy do you make it for your colleagues to find work meaningful and to feel that what they do is important?

3. Develop others to lead

If you have the vision and values correct, if people live and breathe them and consider their work meaningful and important, then you will see people wanting to step up, to show initiative, and to develop themselves and others further, because they are inspired and nurtured by the environment in which they work. Autonomy and self-direction make for much more satisfying work and better workers.

4. Think about what today's mission field looks like

This is one for faith leaders. Bearing in mind my comments about physical and spiritual malnourishment, I'm going to be controversial and suggest that increasingly we need look no further than our own doorstep when thinking about how we may serve as a church. I am struck by the irony of exporting middle-class white saviours to parts of the world that we decide need our help, when we ourselves are living in a spiritual desert. Maybe we could do some kind of exchange scheme, whereby we send people to the developing world to address the challenge of physical famine and, in return, we get help from those who have a simple, uncomplicated faith and live a meaningful and happy life, to help us with our spiritual famine.

Think also about what it means to follow Jesus's great commission in the modern world. A missionary standing on a rock in the middle of the jungle reading out the Gospel in a language incomprehensible to those gathered to stare curiously at them was not likely to be effective or long-lived, particularly if those gathered carried poison arrows, or were considering expanding their culinary repertoire to include this funny-looking long pig. The modern-day equivalent is standing in the market square on a Saturday afternoon hurling the Gospel uninvited at random passers-by. In my view this is likely to be at best ineffective and, in the worst case, may result in harm to your own wellbeing, instigated by those who are just about willing to tolerate buskers, but draw the line at being shouted at by God-botherers when they're out shopping and minding their own business.

Crowds followed Jesus everywhere because they were hungry, physically and spiritually. He didn't have to drum up trade. They saw in him someone who could offer them hope and meet their needs. If one of the purposes of your church is to serve your community, how is that best done where you live? Where are the gaps in local services? Which groups are most in need? Do you have the right people and skills in place to meet those needs? Do you need to make changes within your organization to develop new roles and retire some old ones? Having a shared vision that your team and congregation have bought into will enable you to shake off anything, or anyone, that hinders it. Remember that if you do what you've always done, then you'll get what you've always got.

In conclusion

Just as a good night's sleep, keeping moving, eating well, relaxing, and connecting with others are not optional extras but key elements of wellbeing, so is having meaning and purpose in your life. For many people the easiest and most natural way of having such a framework is having faith. Of course, you can be a spiritual person without necessarily signing up to a particular code of values and conduct.

As the sign that I'd like to put up in large letters outside every church in the land would say: 'You don't have to believe in God to enjoy a meaningful existence, but it helps.' Just because faith makes you happy doesn't mean it isn't also powerful and true. I'm not deluded enough to believe that, after less than half a century of living on this earth, there is one neat answer to life, the universe, and everything for each one of us. One thing I am certain of, though: we all need to explore what this means. Instead of running away from this big, scary question we need to welcome it, face it, and sit with it. So that in the end we can come up with something that's better than '42'.

Notes

1. E.S. Kim, J.K. Sun, N. Park, L.D. Kubzansky, and C. Peterson, 'Purpose in Life and Reduced Risk of Myocardial Infarction among Older U.S. Adults with Coronary Heart Disease: A Two-year Follow-up', *Journal of Behavioral Medicine*, 36: 2: (2013), 124–133.

2. E.S. Kim, J.K. Sun, N. Park, C. Peterson, 'Purpose in Life and Reduced iIncidence of Stroke in Older Adults: The Health and Retirement Study', *Journal of Psychosomatic Research*, 74: 5 (2013), 427–432.

3. A.P. Wingo, T.S. Wingo, W. Fan, et al., 'Purpose in Life is a Robust Protective Factor of Reported Cognitive Decline among Late Middle-aged Adults: The Emory Healthy Aging Study', *Journal of Affective Disorders*, 263 (2020), 310–317.

4. Jim Collins and Jerry I. Porras, *Built to Last: Successful Habits of Visionary Companies* (Random House Business, 2005).

5. A.T. Jebb, L. Tay, E. Diener, *et al.*, 'Happiness, Income Satiation and Turning Points around the World', *Nature Human Behaviour* 2 (2018), 33–38.

6. Tim Jackson, *Prosperity without Growth: Economics for a finite Planet* (London: Earthscan, 2009).

7. N. Spencer, G. Madden, C. Purtill, and J. Ewing, *Religion and Wellbeing: Assessing the Evidence*, 2016. Available at: https://www.theosthinktank.co.uk/cmsfiles/archive/files/Reports/Executive%20Religion%20and%20well-being%20combined%201.pdf.

8. S. Li, M.J. Stampfer, D.R. Williams, and T.J. VanderWeele, 'Association of Religious Service Attendance with Mortality among Women', *JAMA Internal Medicine*, 176: 6 (2016), 777–785.

9. G. Lucchetti, A.L. Lucchetti, and H.G. Koenig, 'Impact of Spirituality/Religiosity on Mortality: Comparison with Other Health Interventions', *Explore (NY)*, 7: 4 (2011 Jul–Aug), 234-238.

10. G. Ironson, H. Kremer, and A. Lucette, 'Relationship between Spiritual Coping and Survival in Patients with HIV', *Journal of General Internal Medicine*, 31: 9 (2015), 1068–1076.

10. PURPOSE AND MEANING

11. Making Changes

For God gave us a spirit not of fear but of power and love and self-control. (2 Timothy 1:7, ESV)

So far, we have covered all the important aspects of wellbeing: sleep, nutrition, movement, relaxation, connection, and purpose. By now you're probably raring to go, having chosen one or more of the tips I have prescribed at the end of each chapter, and maybe having had some ideas of your own too. I can sense your enthusiasm, your impatience to be off on your wellbeing journey. So why, instead of waving you off cheerfully at the end of Chapter 10, have I thrown in this extra one? It's because if I have learnt anything from my personal and professional experience, it's that there's a big difference between knowing the *what*, the *why*, and the *how*.

Moving from what to why to how

If all that was required for us all to make great decisions and lead healthy, happy lives full of purpose was simply information, then there'd be no problem. There'd be much less need for the medical profession and for social services. You wouldn't be reading this book because, as I have already admitted, nothing in here is rocket science. The Government might send you a text or an email update every few years, just as a reminder. You would have heard it all before and be practising it to flawless perfection. There'd be no obesity or mental health crises. We'd all be enjoying great quality of life, whichever score was used to measure it.

But we're not there. We're still here. Let's be clear: pretty much everyone knows the *what*. A random sample of most people in the High Street will reveal that they know that sleep is really important, that we should eat more vegetables, be physically active, drink alcohol in moderation, not smoke, set aside some time to relax and promote good mental health, have good relationships, and even take time to contemplate the deep and meaningful from time to time. So why aren't we all doing it?

Most people are also fairly comfortable with the *why*; that is, why these things are important. You, for example, may now know more about stress and inflammation as the common soil of disease, based on what you have read in this book. You may be comfortable with the concept of the anti-inflammatory properties of these various lifestyle measures that are likely to benefit you and promote a good lifespan and healthspan.

The problem is with the *how*. This is where so many of us come unstuck.

· · ·

The purpose of this final chapter is to consider change. Not just how we deal with it passively, but how we instigate and manage it actively. How we can turn it from something scary that happens to us into something that we actively seek out, embrace, take control of, and use for good, both for ourselves and others.

There are plenty of excellent books out there on behavioural psychology and how to apply it to make successful changes. You may wish to explore the topic to gain deeper understanding. I recommend *Nudge* by Richard Thaler and Cass Sunstein,[1] *Think Small* by Owain Service and Rory Gallagher,[2] and *Tiny Habits* by B.J. Fogg.[3] For now you will have to content yourself with my having taken all that I have learnt from reading, listening, discussing with others, and putting into practice in my own life over the last few years, and distilling it down into my final prescription for you at the end of this chapter. Before we go there, first of all let's think a bit about change.

Change is inevitable

As Heraclitus said, 'Change is the only constant in life'. Life itself is a process of constant change whether at the microscopic level, with the birth and death of the cells in our body every moment of our existence, or at the macroscopic level across our society, our nations, and our planet over time. Even if you were to do your absolute best not to change anything at all about your life in any way, all the different factors that determine the environment around you would make this impossible.

Depending on where you are in life and even just what sort of day you are having, change can be threatening, encouraging, or even inspiring. Whichever of these is the case, it is also usually at least a little uncomfortable. I recommend you both expect it and accept it. Just imagine being strapped into a rollercoaster as it gets pulled slowly to the highest point of the ride. You've signed up to the deal. You can't stop it, but you can relax into it. As you plunge into the vertiginous drop, would you rather be screaming in fear or excitement?

Change is desirable

As I've said before, we are made to be in motion in every aspect of our lives whether physical, emotional, or spiritual. In the words of George Bernard Shaw: 'Progress is impossible without change and those who cannot change their minds cannot change anything.'

Change is often driven by pain. It stimulates us to do life differently. If you are unhappy with the way that things are going, you are going to need a different plan if you want a different life. Darwin pointed out that the species that survived were not necessarily the strongest or the most intelligent, but those that were the most responsive to change.

So instead of fearing change, we should embrace it. We should actively plan for change, thinking about what the changes are we would like to make, instead of waiting for them to happen to us. We should seek change even (or especially) when things are going well, rather than thinking of change as being something that you only do reluctantly when forced to. One of the benefits of this is that the resilient mindset we build as a result of managing change successfully will stand us in good stead for the rest of our lives, whatever the challenges we face and the reasons for them.

Change comes from within

In Chapter 8, on stress and relaxation, I wrote about the importance of focusing on what you can control. We can only make changes in those areas, which gives us both power and responsibility. That said, it isn't just about willpower. Again, if this was all that was required for successful change, then we wouldn't have a problem. Environment is a recurrent theme here. One of the reasons that we aren't all perfect, healthy beings, living perfectly logical lives (apart from the fact that we are human, of course) is that we have been shaped by the environment around us, even before birth. Many forces, some of them malevolent, are at play in what we have accepted as our default norms when it comes to what we eat, how much we move, how we interact with others, and so on.

'Lifestyle medicine' is a term disliked by some, who feel it suggests that we have all made conscious choices and therefore deserve to be blamed if things haven't turned out well for us. It's certainly too simplistic to say this is all about willpower. As human beings we are a collection of habits as much as we are a collection of microorganisms. Our habits, the little things that we do every day, consume the majority of our time and make us complicated. Big changes can be hard to effect because there isn't just one lever to pull.

The upside of our being complex creatures composed of habits is that we can take back control, one bit at a time. We may not be personally able to control the availability of junk food and price of alcohol where we live, the effectiveness of our public transport system, or wellbeing policies at our place of work (although it is worth considering how we might influence those things as a more powerful collective), but we can fight back by resetting our own internal defaults and deciding what we want our new normals to be. We can make small changes in our lives and benefit from incremental gains.

By changing our habits, we can actually change *who* we are. It's not a question of putting on a show or pretending to be something we are not. Achieving even just one small success allows us to perceive ourselves differently, which in turn will motivate us to make even more successful changes. Instead of labelling themselves as 'fat' or 'unfit', a person can see themselves as someone who is currently carrying excess weight and taking steps to become more physically active. A friend of mine was not happy with her levels of activity and fitness, and so decided to do the Couch to 5k programme. Her progress was slow and steady, interrupted by accidents and injuries, but she persisted. Even by the end of the programme, when she was able to run 5k without stopping, she still insisted that she was not a runner. Then she started doing Parkrun every week. Now when we chat after the weekend, we usually talk about how her Parkrun went. She even does two on the same day when the Parkrun calendar permits. She has stopped protesting when I call her a runner, because now she is, however fast or slowly she does it, and she knows it.

I've already said that if you want a different life you need a different plan. You can't do this by remaining where you are. You must be prepared to give up what you currently perceive yourself to be, so that you can become what you want to be.

What can we learn about making changes from the Bible?

We needn't fear change

> For God gave us a spirit not of fear but of power and love and self-control. (2 Timothy 1: 7, ESV)

Rather than being paralysed by fear, we can start to take back control of our lives even in the midst of what may feel like chaos. The more we do this, the more powerful it makes us. We should show kindness and love to ourselves, as we would to others, when working through what may be a difficult process. The better the system we design for ourselves, the more likely we are to succeed. Success builds more success.

We shouldn't be afraid to ask for help.

> Plans fail for lack of counsel but with many advisers they succeed. (Proverbs 15: 22, NIV)

Are there people in your life that can advise and support you when it comes to making changes? They might be able to help as you develop an understanding of the challenges that you face, determine your priorities, and make your plan. They can encourage you and hold you accountable as you put it into action.

We should make ourselves accountable to God, as we do to others

> Commit to the Lord whatever you do and he will establish your plans. (Proverbs 16: 3, NIV)

It may be that you don't need a revelation from God to come up with a plan to eat fewer doughnuts and go for a walk each day. We are after all autonomous, thinking beings with minds of our own. That said, one of the principles of behaviour change is that of accountability. If the scientific evidence shows that we are more likely to succeed if we declare our intentions to our friends, family, or colleagues in order for them to support and encourage us, why would we not include our creator for that extra layer of accountability?

We don't have to do it all by ourselves (but we do have to do it).

> I can do all things through him who strengthens me. (Philippians 4: 13, ESV)

Taking on a new challenge and making a change isn't easy or painless. It will require effort and grit. God isn't going to smite you with a lightning bolt should you stray from the narrow path of kale-covered salvation to the broad path of damnation, paved with pizza. Nor is he going to do the heavy lifting for you. We can't outsource motivation or momentum to the Almighty. You could opt to pray for a miraculous cure for your diabetes without any weight loss whatsoever, or for a resolution for your depression without doing any self-care. This is likely to work about as well as someone sitting in a burning building praying to be rescued, instead of walking out of the fire exit right in front of them.

What God does do is strengthen us. Having a relationship with God enables us to do more for ourselves than we ever thought possible, like the coach who helps you lift more, run further and faster, or achieve a personal goal you never thought was possible.

God's word is there to guide us

Everything in the Scriptures is God's Word. All of it is useful for teaching and helping people and for correcting them and showing them how to live.
(2 Timothy 3: 16f, CEV)

I have yet to find the chapter in the Bible that contains a ten-point plan for getting promotion, running a marathon in under two hours, or making that tricky second album. Even as a follower of the Christian faith I sometimes struggle to discern the relevance of particular passages to life in the contemporary world. However, once you accept the Bible isn't a textbook or technical manual, there are plenty of principles there to guide us. On the one hand, our lives may seem extraordinarily complex, yet on the other, it's only this way because we make it so. It's this overcomplication which is causing us problems and we end up getting in our own way.

To really get the most out of life, to live the way that we are meant to, we need to get back to basics. I hope that the way I have structured this book, referring back to scripture as part of each chapter, has been a helpful illustration of this. God's word is a lamp for our feet and a light on our path. If we make decisions that conflict directly with these teachings, with the basic principles of what it means to live a happy and meaningful life, then we need to ask ourselves whether we are still on the right path.

Make the most of what you've got

Teach us to number our days, that we may gain a heart of wisdom. (Psalm 90: 12, NIV)

One of the reasons that we don't make good decisions in the moment is because we aren't thinking about the long term and the bigger picture, but are concerned with short-term gratification. Numbering our days doesn't mean just counting them, but also considering how we make the best use of the talents and resources that we have been given, however modest they may be. What are we devoting our time to? Are we spending it wisely and being productive? What do we want for the future?

We all have different capacities and capabilities. God doesn't necessarily demand that we get an 'A' for attainment, but we can all get one for effort.

Every day is a fresh start

Create in me a clean heart, O God, and renew a right spirit within me. (Psalm 51: 10, ESV)

The past is past. Making one simple change can be the start of the process of transforming your entire life. You don't need to be weighed down by the baggage of the person that you were yesterday. If this applies to those that don't believe, think about how much more this applies if you have a relationship with God. No matter how well or how badly yesterday or today went, each new day and each new moment is an opportunity to be transformed.

My prescription for making successful changes

So here it is, my final prescription of top tips – is that a sigh of relief I can hear? I've been saving the best for last. This time I'm not differentiating between individuals and organizations, as the principles translate broadly between both groups.

1. Ask yourself whether you are ready to change

It's not a question of whether you need to (most of us do) or whether it would make other people happy, but whether you are ready to. If you aren't, right now, be honest with yourself and others and don't waste anyone's time, including your own. Change can be tough enough even when you are ready for it. If you're not, it's an absolute showstopper, a do-not-pass-go moment. You may be in what is described as the 'pre-contemplative' phase in the cycle of change: not yet thinking about it, and definitely not yet ready. I see this a lot with people who aren't yet ready to quit smoking, drink less or eat differently. That's absolutely fine.

May I just make one plea? Don't complain about the problems in your life that persist or worsen as a result of your active decision not to change. Remember the person in the burning building with a fire exit right in front of them? Just come back when you're ready.

2. Think about the why as well as the what

Our motivation can be *extrinsic* (coming from outside of us, usually related to wanting a reward or avoiding a punishment), or *intrinsic* (coming from inside us, doing something we enjoy for its own sake). Both have their place. A goal can be achieved in different ways, taking different approaches. Imagine a person who is overweight. They might decide to lose weight because their doctor has told them they need to. They sign up to Weight Watchers because it will make them accountable and they want to win Slimmer of the Week, and to avoid shame. These are examples of extrinsic motivation.

Someone else with the same weight issues might decide for themselves that they want to lose weight because they would like to be able to run around in the park with their grandkids. Their approach to this is to empty their cupboards of junk food, reduce their portion size, and go for more walks with their friends, which they enjoy anyway. This is more intrinsically motivated.

In my experience, most people do better in the long term when they are intrinsically motivated. However, external motivation does work for some people, particularly when stopping one habit or taking up a new one is initially tougher (e.g. quitting smoking). Always ask yourself why you want to do something, asking yourself the same question in response to each answer until you have stripped it right back to your core motivation for change.

3. Start small

Like all the other doses of medicine, whether lifestyle- or pill-related, behaviour change should be taken in the right dose. I believe that behaviour change also has a dose-response curve. The more goals, the more complex, the more likely you are to fail to achieve some or all of them. The simpler your goal, the lower the bar you set, the more likely you are to achieve it. The more you achieve, the more encouraged you will be, and the more likely you are to sustain your new behaviour and to build on it, taking on greater challenges which you are now better equipped to do.

Success leads on to more success. You might want to run a marathon, having never run in your life. Start with getting off the couch, putting on your shoes, and jogging to the end of the road. The right goal will make you feel stretched (after all, if it doesn't challenge you, it won't change you), but not to the point where you snap.

4. Break it down

If the change you would like to make is large or complex then, in keeping with the last point, I recommend you try breaking it down into smaller components. This is partly because having a smaller goal is easier to achieve, and partly because sometimes it's necessary to understand what the individual steps are that all have to be successful to achieve the overall change you want. Let's say, for example, that I want to take up archery after watching the Olympics. I can't just turn up with a bow and arrows in my local park and take pot shots at the scenery. I would need to find the nearest club that ran training sessions on days I could make, complete a beginner's course, and then sign up to pay the necessary fees before eventually buying my own equipment. I would also then need to commit to regular practice to progress and get the most enjoyment out of it, which in turn means I would be more likely to stick with it.

Breaking it down beforehand gives you the opportunity to check whether this is something you can definitely commit to, and also to anticipate where the roadblocks might be (such as time commitment or expense), which you can then hopefully work around.

5. Set up the environment and create your own norms

I have referred repeatedly to the problems with living in an environment where the default settings have been determined by others and are largely beyond our control. The good news is that we can fight back by creating our own environment with defaults and values that we set. You can control what sort of food you keep in your cupboards, what time you go to bed and get up, which days you work, and which days or times you set aside for rest. You can set defaults for Wi-Fi connectivity, apps, notifications, and screen time on your mobile device (and those of your children). You can use physical prompts each day, such as your yoga mat by the TV, your running shoes in front of the door, or your Bible by your bedside.

You can anchor something that you want to become a habit onto something else that already is one. I leave weights on my desk, in front of my computer, so that I remember to use them each morning before I write. You could practise gratitude or do some squats as you wait for the kettle to boil each morning. Eventually these activities will become automatic and you can always build on that or mix in other ones to avoid getting bored.

6. Reward yourself to develop a habit

A related aspect of setting up your environment for success is how you will reward yourself for certain behaviours. Now some will, of course, have their own reward. Enjoying a nice afternoon's shooting with your archery club in the sunshine is probably enough in itself. In fact, rewarding people for things that they already like doing is at best pointless and at worst may diminish the enjoyment and motivation they feel. However, for bigger, more challenging changes there is a place for 'temptation bundling' as part of extrinsic motivation. This means associating something you really like with the behaviour that you are introducing. For example, my wife treats herself to an episode of one of her favourite Netflix series when using our treadmill; an activity which she would otherwise consider very boring.

It used to be thought that the key to developing habits was simply to do something repeatedly. There is an element of truth to this. However, enjoyment has a much more potent habit-forming effect. Habits are likely to stick quicker if you find them rewarding.

7. *Make a plan*

I strongly encourage my patients and clients to have a written-down plan, which puts together all the components that I have listed here in this prescription. It's an essential part of our consultations together. It doesn't need to be set in stone. Your goal, and the individual steps you have broken it down into, may change. The best-laid plans are the ones that are flexible and responsive to your needs. One of the benefits of having a plan, whether electronic or a hard copy, is that you can remind yourself of it regularly and also share it with others.

8. *Make yourself accountable*

If you are brave enough to share your plans, you might want to appoint someone to be your referee. It might be a friend, family member, work colleague, mentor, or leader in your faith community. You are giving this person permission to support you, to ask you how it's going, and even to challenge you when necessary. This might take the form of regularly touching base in the morning at work, or at home at the end of the day. Perhaps a message sent at whatever intervals you agree between you? It depends on what the change is that you are making.

If you are considering this, pick your referee carefully. The ideal referee is a bit like a mattress – the right mix of supportive and firm. You don't want someone who is either going to collude with you or make your life miserable. For that reason, your spouse or partner may be either the very first or very last person that you would ask to take on this role. I'll leave that one with you!

9. Be kind to yourself

Just as it was once said that all political careers end in failure, so it is highly likely that at one stage or another of a grand wellbeing plan, the wheels may come off. Don't beat yourself up. Making changes isn't easy. You may not get it right the first time. It isn't all or nothing. It doesn't mean that you weren't right to try. Life can be painful enough without unnecessary self-flagellation. Instead of viewing it as a personal failure, view it as a failure of the system you set up. This creates an opportunity to learn and improve. Nothing is entirely wasted. The person who never makes a mistake never learns anything. Consider it part of your foundation which you build on for success. Come up with a new plan and go again.

10. Stick with it

This last tip is really an accumulation of all of the others. It's cheating slightly, but I wanted to have a nice round top ten of tips, so I'm allowing it. The point here is that there are many different aspects of behaviour change to consider in making something stick. There is no one guaranteed recipe for success. You may start with an epiphany, as you leap out of the bath shouting 'eureka!' Motivation provides the starting gun for change. Without motivation, nothing can happen. But just as a spark ignites an engine, fuel is then needed to keep it running.

Planning, breaking it down, starting small, setting your environment for success, rewarding yourself, and making yourself accountable all increase your chances, not just of initially achieving this change but, ultimately, of sustaining it, which is what it's all about. Being kind to yourself, learning from your mistakes, and going again are all part of developing resilience, grit, and stickability in you as a person, as well as developing your plan.

That's the end of my prescription for making successful changes. In fact, that's the end of all my prescriptions in this book. I have one more suggestion to make before you turn over to the conclusion. It may be that you have been particularly struck by some of the tips and suggestions from the previous chapters. You may have made some notes or highlighted parts of the text. If you haven't got around to doing this yet, may I encourage you to do this now? In writing this book it has always been my intention and hope that when you have finished reading it, you don't just think 'hmm, interesting' and put it on a shelf or coffee table, but that you use it as a jumping-off point to consider your wellbeing and what changes you might like to make to aspects of your life, whether physical, mental, or spiritual.

Why not make a brief list of the ideas that you would like to explore and consider how you would incorporate them into a personal or collective Wellbeing Plan? I've included a template for you to use or adapt as you wish just below. There's no time like the present. Take advantage of this eureka moment. You are only ever one step away from living life better.

My wellbeing plan

- What does living life well mean to me?

- What changes would I like to make?

- What goals will I set myself to make these changes? (Be specific.)

- What are the steps I need to take to achieve each goal? (Break it down for each goal, think about how to avoid potential roadblocks.)

- Who could support me and hold me accountable?

- How will I know if I have achieved these goals?

- What has gone well and what might I do differently next time?

Notes

1. Richard Thaler and Cass R. Sunstein, *Nudge: Improving Decisions About Health, Wealth, and Happiness* (New Haven: Yale University Press, 2008).

2. Owain Service and Rory Gallagher, *Think Small: The Surprisingly Simple Ways to Reach Big Goals* (Michael O' Mara, 2018).

3. B.J. Fogg, *Tiny Habits: The Small Changes that Change Everything* (Boston: Houghton Mifflin Harcourt, 2020).

12. Wellbeing wound up

Now we're at the end, let's remind ourselves how we began. I asked you some questions about how well you felt, how satisfied you were with life, what was important to you, whether you had the right balance of physical, mental, and spiritual wellbeing, and what living life better would look like to you. Depending on how long it's taken you to read this book, that might have been anywhere from a few hours to a few weeks ago. It might be a little too soon for your entire life to have changed! My hope is that you have asked yourself questions you haven't considered before, and given yourself time to reflect on the answers in a way that you might not have done before either. Maybe you now have a short list – or even a long one – of the ideas that have struck you, and of the wellbeing tips I have prescribed which are relevant to you.

My hope and prayer for you is not that this book will change your life, but that it will be the catalyst for you deciding what you want to change and starting that process. My intention was to keep it broad, simple, and pragmatic. You may now want to go deeper into some areas. Get stuck in. Read, listen, discuss. This kind of learning is more likely to endure and enable you to share with others.

Time for a quick recap

I'd like to imagine that you will of course have memorized every line of scribbled wit and wisdom contained within this book, incorporated all the best bits into a comprehensive wellbeing plan that you have already laminated and stuck on your wall, and that any kind of recap is really quite unnecessary for someone like you. So, these selected highlights are for those other people who may not be quite as advanced. Just humour me for a few more paragraphs. It's also an exercise in the discipline of *being short and to the point*, as I really distil it down.

Sleep

We are designed to sleep. It's fundamental to restoration and repair, for mind and body. Most of us need more than we think. This applies to you if you usually either feel tired in the morning or are woken by your alarm. Consistently choosing chronic sleep deprivation is more masochistic than macho, a form of slow euthanasia. You need the right dose. Good sleep hygiene is key. Prepare properly for sleep. Being well-slept is performance-enhancing and means we are doing life better before we have even got out of bed in the morning. Seek help if you are concerned there may be underlying reasons for poor sleep.

Food

Food is medicine. You need the right dose. Don't get sucked into the Diet Wars. Remember that the best diet is not a diet, but is simple, affordable, balanced, and flexible. Eat real food, mainly plants (a good source of antioxidants, which will reduce inflammation), not too much. Avoid highly processed food. Eating fewer carbohydrates (beige, starchy food) will work better than a low-fat, calorie-counting approach for some people. Be kind to yourself. No one is perfect. Everything in moderation, including moderation. People also need to be fed physically in order to grow spiritually.

Movement

It's both our natural state and a miracle drug. By putting movement back in its rightful place in your life you can overcome Movement Deficiency Disorder and make your escape from the toxic death cult of convenience. You need the right dose. Start small, do more. Choose something enjoyable and meaningful. Keeping moving means you will live longer, age better, and enjoy a good healthspan. Don't give up. Physical and spiritual discipline are two sides of the same coin. Run with endurance the race that is set before you.

A renewed mind

Stress isn't good or bad. We need some in our lives. What matters is the dose and our response to it. Move out of the fast lane and give yourself time and space every day, even if it's just for a few minutes. It's a good investment, which will allow you to deal better with life. Practise gratitude, enjoy nature, nurture relationships, think positively, focus on what you can control, be realistic and kind to yourself. Practising mindfulness helps you to live an intentional, less distracted life. Consider decluttering your life physically and digitally.

Don't artificially separate the physical from the mental from the spiritual. Do your own Sabbath. God rested; so should we.

Connections

We all need connections, again in the right dose. We are stronger in a group. Being alone is not the same as being lonely. Loneliness is a part of life and nothing to be feared in the short term. There are signs that it is growing, particularly amongst the elderly and young adults. Key factors might be the cult of personal freedom and losing our religion. Remember the blue zone principles of belonging to a community, putting your loved ones first, and developing the right social circle for mutual support. Make sure your relationship with technology doesn't compromise your relationships with others. Ask for help and give it too. God cares for the lonely and so should we, whatever our belief system.

Meaning and purpose

It's in our nature to seek out purpose and meaning in life. Being all we can be, looking beyond ourselves to see the bigger picture and help others is part of our hierarchy of needs. Having purpose in life, including the practice of an active faith, improves not just your mental and spiritual health, but your physical health too. We all have a way of doing life, and rules we live by, whether we realize this or not. Set aside time to consider your purpose, your *ikigai*. Think about how you view your work. Remember the happiness equation. An active and meaningful faith will result in both improved wellbeing for the individual, and a meaningful impact within the community served by groups that share these values.

Making changes

Change is an inevitable consequence of being alive. Instead of reacting reluctantly to it being thrust upon you, you can plan it positively and proactively. Expect it to be stretching, even a little uncomfortable, as this is necessary to grow and develop resilience. Change starts from within: you may not be able to change the external environment, so consider what you can control and what norms you can set for yourself. Be honest with yourself about whether you're ready. Think not just about the *what*, but the *why* and the *how*. Start small. Break it down. Make a plan. Make yourself accountable. Reward and be kind to yourself. Learn from failure. Stick with it.

• • •

There, that wasn't too bad was it? I like to think of this book as a simple place to start from, accessible to everyone and anyone. That said, when going back through it as part of the editing process I realized that I've packed quite a lot into it. I wouldn't blame you for feeling a little overwhelmed and perhaps suffering from lifestyle-medicine-induced indigestion. I often feel that myself when I read or listen to something that goes beyond what I am already confident in and familiar with.

I recently found myself halfway through a two-hour podcast focused entirely on breathing techniques, and realized that I had lost both my bearings and my will to live. So, I want to encourage you not to sweat the small stuff. There may be a place for debating the relative merits of low versus very low carb diets, or the utility of alternate nostril breathing, but I would suggest that it's at the very top end of the dose-response curve, in the land of marginal gains.

Most of us will never want or need to get into this level of detail, because there are massive gains to be enjoyed just from starting with the small stuff. For you it might be going to bed an hour earlier and turning your phone off, or taking the first few steps off the couch and down the street. It could be eating more vegetables and less highly processed food; or maybe your plan is to find five minutes a day to practise gratitude, or rest and meditate. Perhaps your priority is considering your relationships and your purpose in life. You might be considering how to use the principles of behaviour change to do more press-ups each day and eat better, or you might be thinking of applying this to your spiritual practice and developing a better routine when it comes to prayer, meditation, or reading the Bible. Personally, I will take much more satisfaction from a lot of people should be making small changes to their lives than just a few people making big ones.

· · ·

Life is messy. Change is constant. Health and wellbeing are not binary. You are not entirely healthy or unhealthy, either physically or spiritually, but in a state of flux somewhere along the spectrum in between. You won't achieve perfection, so don't worry about trying. Feeling well and living a fulfilling life is not a race with winners and losers. In this respect there is no final destination, only the journey.

My hope and prayer for all of us is that we each discover along the way what it truly means to be 'fit for purpose'.

Acknowledgments

If this book were a recipe, the list of ingredients would be a long one. I'm going to attempt to thank those who helped, in roughly chronological order. If I have missed anyone out, I apologise.

Mum and Dad, thank you for helping me build the foundations for life. Now that I am a parent I realize just how demanding and rewarding this is. You instilled in me the importance of doing my best. I will continue to try. Stew, you are not just my brother but a wise and generous friend. The support we have had as a family from you and Liz has been a real blessing and I look forward to continuing to work with the fantastic team at OneLife, supporting young leaders.

Mike, it's been thirty seven years since we met in 1W. We used to talk about being authors one day. Our theology may be different, but we remain firmly bound by our friendship and our love of reading, tech, and the Red Devils. If you look carefully you will see where you made it into the book.

Al, I don't have words to describe the importance of both your friendship to me and the friendship between our families. Thank you for putting up with my ramblings and being a sounding board over the years, whether hurtling coast to coast on mountain bikes or sitting in a corner of the Plough.

Parkbury House Surgery has been my other family for the last 20 years. It is a pleasure and privilege to work with such a fine team of people. There are too many names to mention but you know who you are, particularly the regulars at the Parkbury Arms.

John Bayliss, we started out as colleagues, became mentor and mentee, and ended up as friends. Thank you for all your support in my cardiology training. Remember our talks about cardiac prehab? They are now bearing fruit. You are the only cardiologist I know who would have made an even better general practitioner. I hope you'll take that as a compliment.

Staypals, it was an immense privilege to be invited to join the group 20 years ago, and I have been more and more grateful for your friendship and support with every passing year. We've had some amazing times over the years. Thank you for letting me try out some of my stuff on the group, admittedly in variable states of sobriety. Remember, it's not a holiday, it's an educational study weekend.

A thankyou goes to my CCG and Public Health colleagues for your support and collaboration in seeing the bigger picture. Working at scale can be slow and difficult but the prize is huge and worth the effort. Honourable mentions to Nicolas Small, David Evans, Kathryn Magson, Piers Simey, Jim McManus, Louise Savory, and Miranda Sutters.

To the Manly Men, past and present, everyone needs a tribe. Thank you for being my mine.

Tim and Jackie, thank you for giving me the opportunity to put my passion into practice by working with Thrive Tribe, an inspiring organisation full of inspiring people.

To Simon, Steve, and the Living Life Better team: we talked the talk, now we're walking the walk. It's always exciting, sometimes a little scary, and the future looks busy.

Teen Daze, your music has been the soundtrack to writing this book. According to Apple Music I listened to *Bioluminescence* almost one hundred times in doing so. Ian Rankin, thank you for introducing me to more great writing music, Pye Corner Audio.

To Rose, Bengono, the rest of the team at Harper Inspire and your colleagues at HarperCollins, thank you for believing in me, giving me this opportunity and guiding me through the process. It appears I'm not crazy after all!

To my agent, Jonathan, thank you for your support, advice and your willingness to answer a lot of probably quite stupid questions. I have plenty more.

There are many people whose work and wisdom has influenced and informed me over the years. You are the giants I referred to in the introduction of this book, whose shoulders I am now standing on. Thanks to Rangan Chatterjee, Aseem Malhotra, Ayan Panja, Donal O'Neill, Stephen Dubner, Daniel Kahneman, Richard Thaler, Mark Hyman, Malcom Kendrick, David Spiegelhalter, David and Jen Unwin, Matthew Walker and John Mark Comer. I have been privileged to get to know some of you but inspired by all of you.

To my patients: I hope that doing my best to put into real-life general practice what I have learnt has, more often than not, been of benefit to you. It certainly has been to me. I will continue to try to do even better.

Finally, once more, thank you to my wife and children. You are at the heart of this book and my life.

Author's Note

Thank you for reading this book. Writing it has been something of a personal mission and to be here now with it complete feels a little strange! My purpose has been not just to inform or entertain (although I hope you've experienced a little of both) but also to challenge, to encourage reflection and to inspire people to live life better. As I said in the introduction, this book won't change your life, but acting on what comes out of reading it might. That's my hope and prayer for you.

I've certainly got a lot out of it myself. Learning from others, digging deeper into research, combining it with my personal and professional experience and somehow putting it all together in a vaguely coherent way has been hard, painstaking, and highly rewarding work. It has changed the way that I do life, inside and outside my consulting room. It has also given me a lot of ideas for what could come next, inside and outside the pages of a book. Avoiding becoming distracted and overexcited by these ideas has been one of my biggest challenges. I've coped by keeping a not-so-little list for a rainy day. So if you're reading this and it's raining, then you'll know what I'm up to.

If you have enjoyed reading this book, please consider spreading the word with a review and sharing it with others. I would also really value your feedback on the book; it will help me to learn, improve and further develop ideas.

If you'd like to stay in touch and keep up to date with the progress of this book and other projects, you can follow me on social media. I can be found on Twitter (@DrRichardPile), Instagram (@ richardpile) and LinkedIn (drrichardpile).

Dr Richard Pile